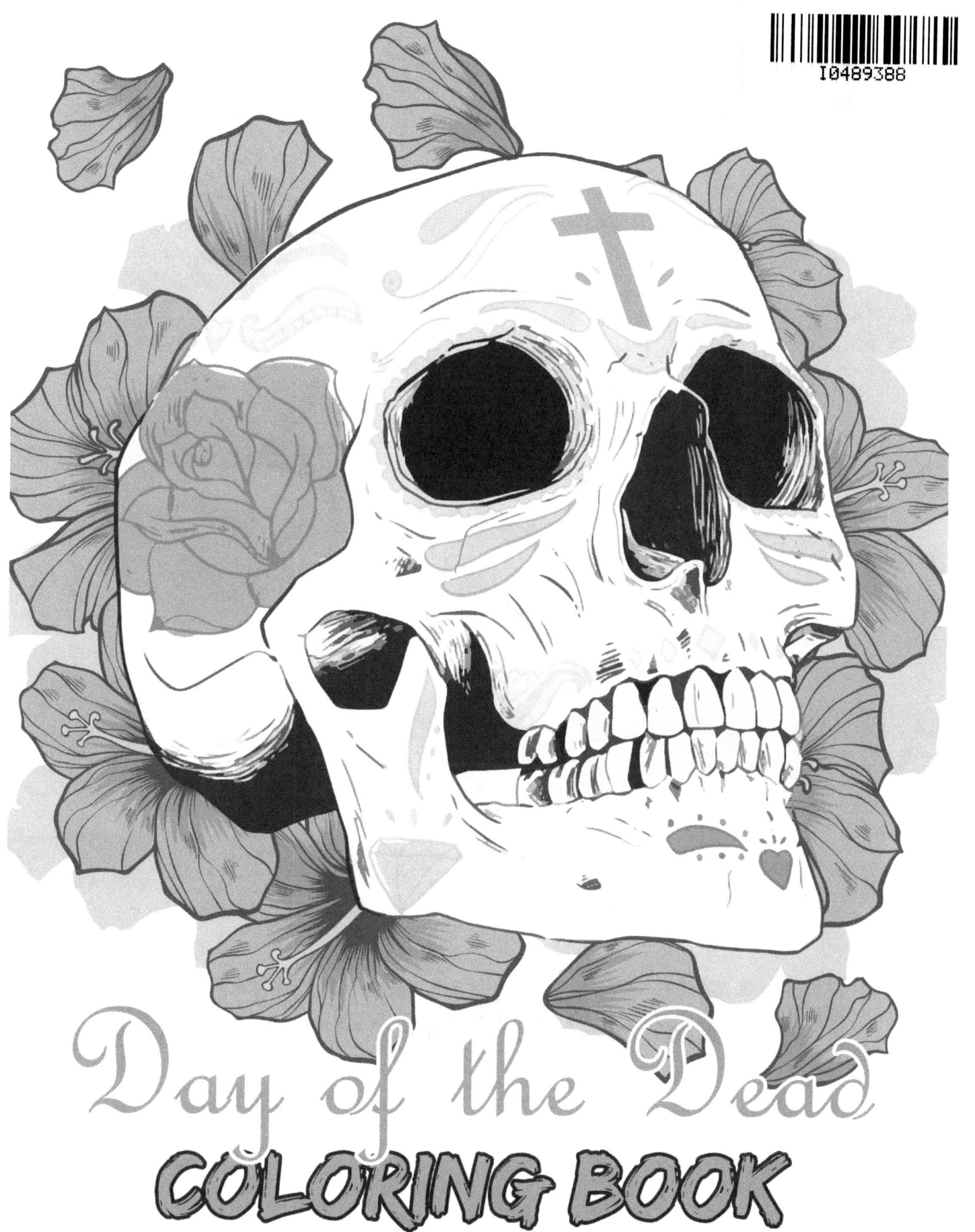

Day of the Dead

COLORING BOOK

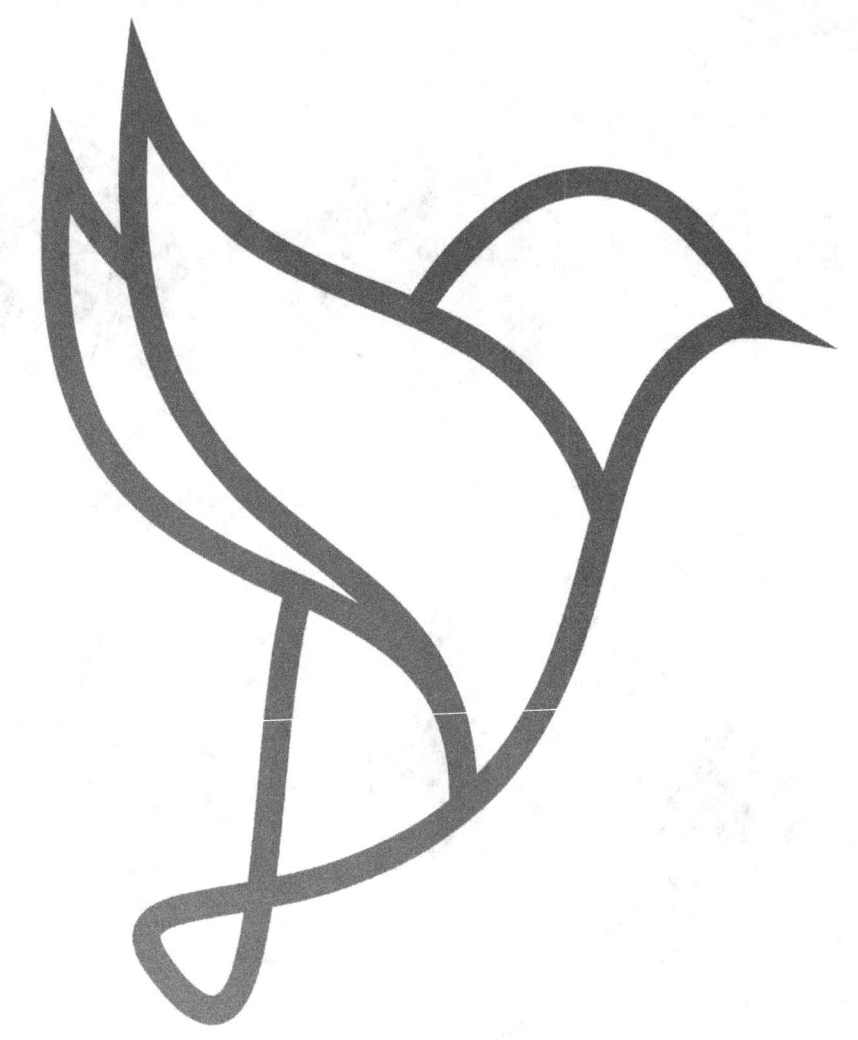

FREEDOMBIRD DESIGN

Published by PUBLISHING COMPANY in 2016

First edition: First printing

Illustrations and design © 2016 author name

Author Contact

https://www.facebook.com/groups/1523056898003358/

ISBN-13: 978-1546613282

ISBN-10: 1546613285

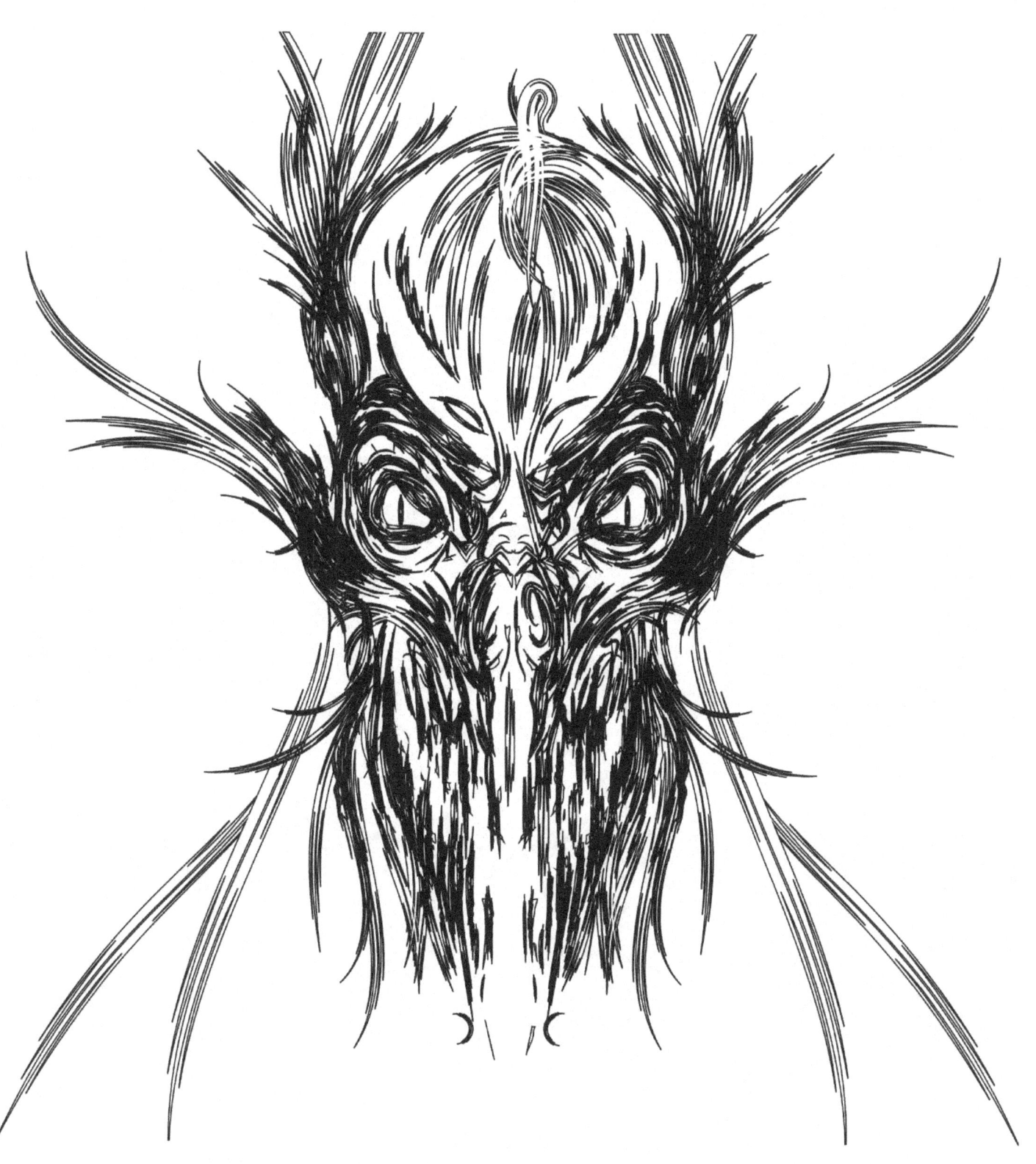

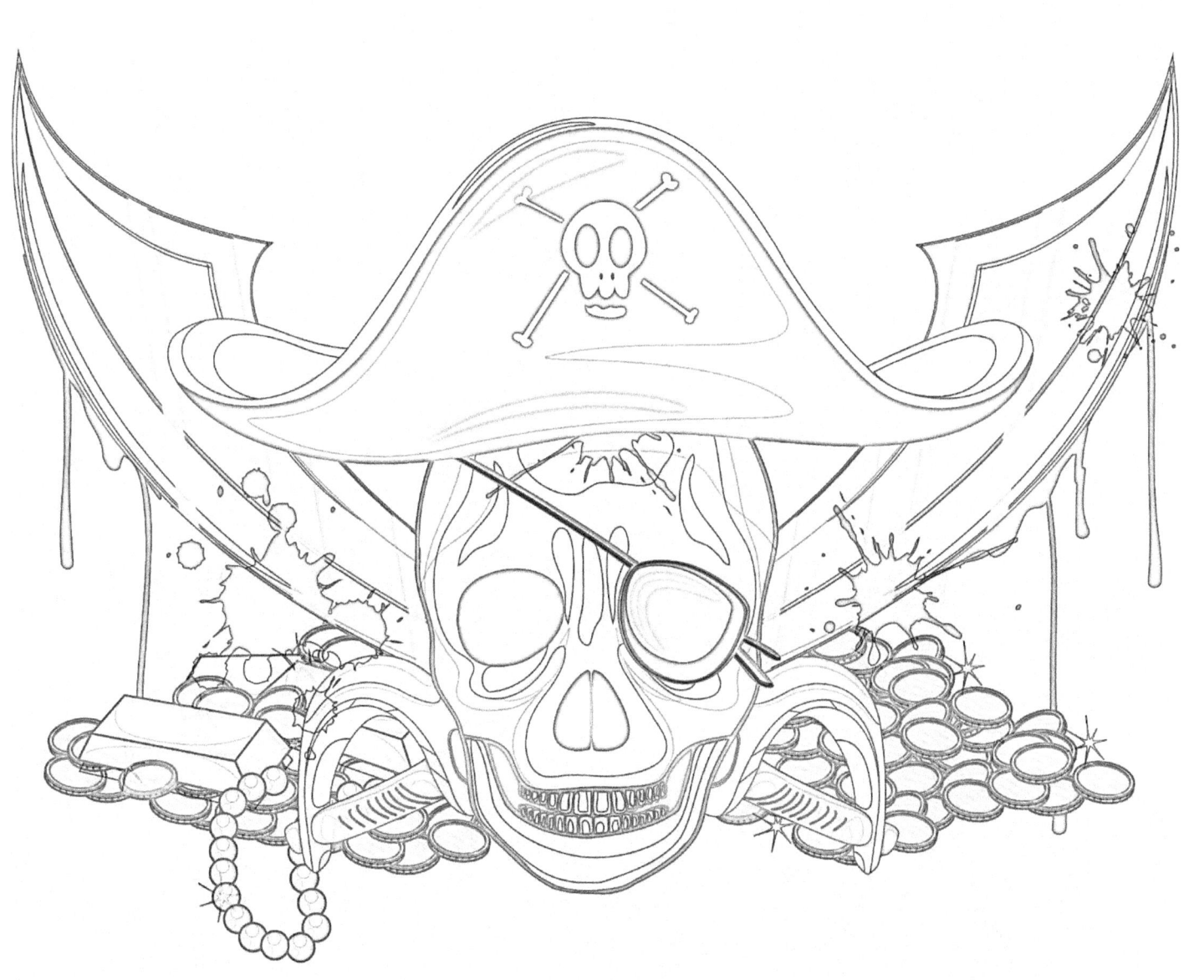

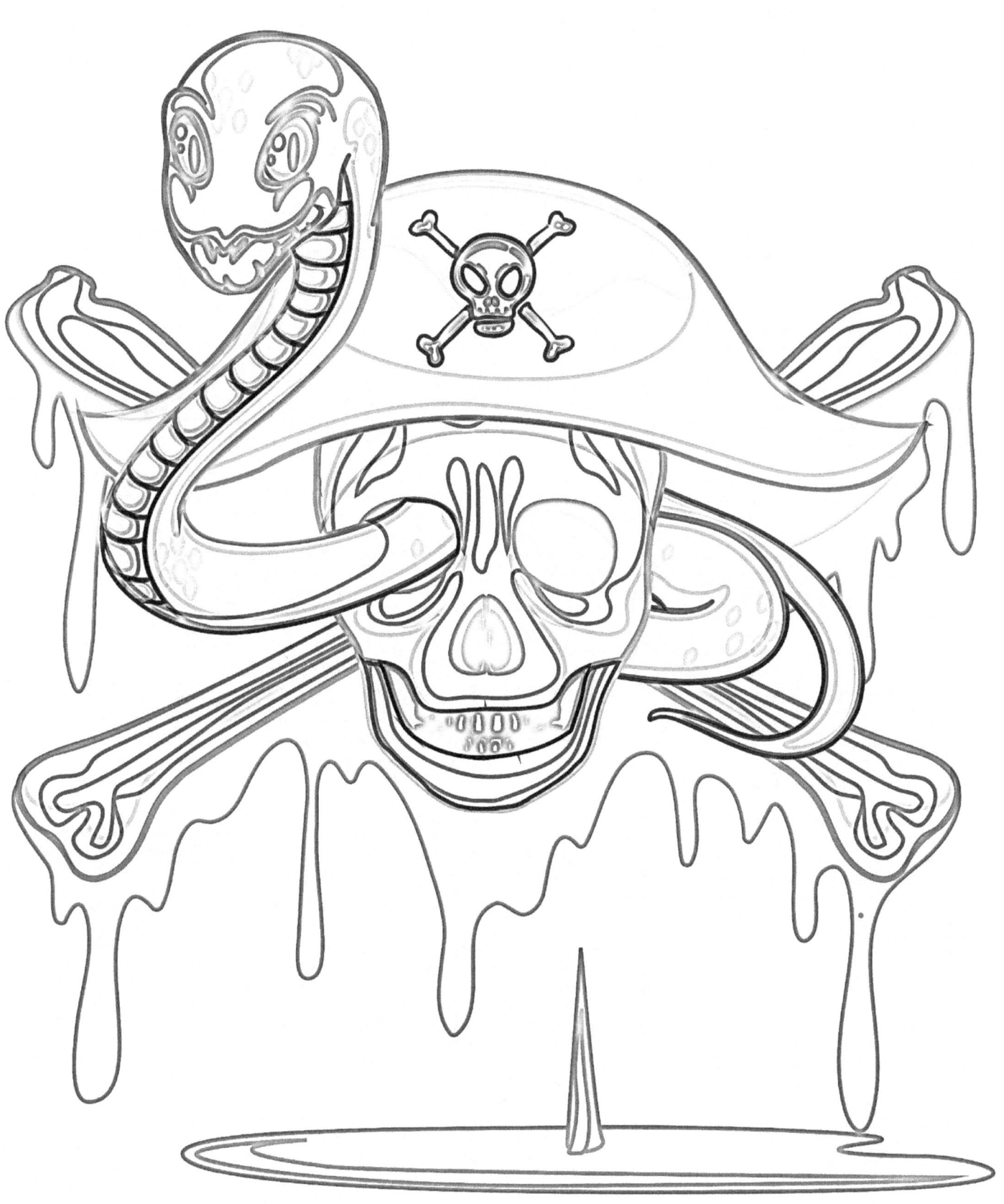

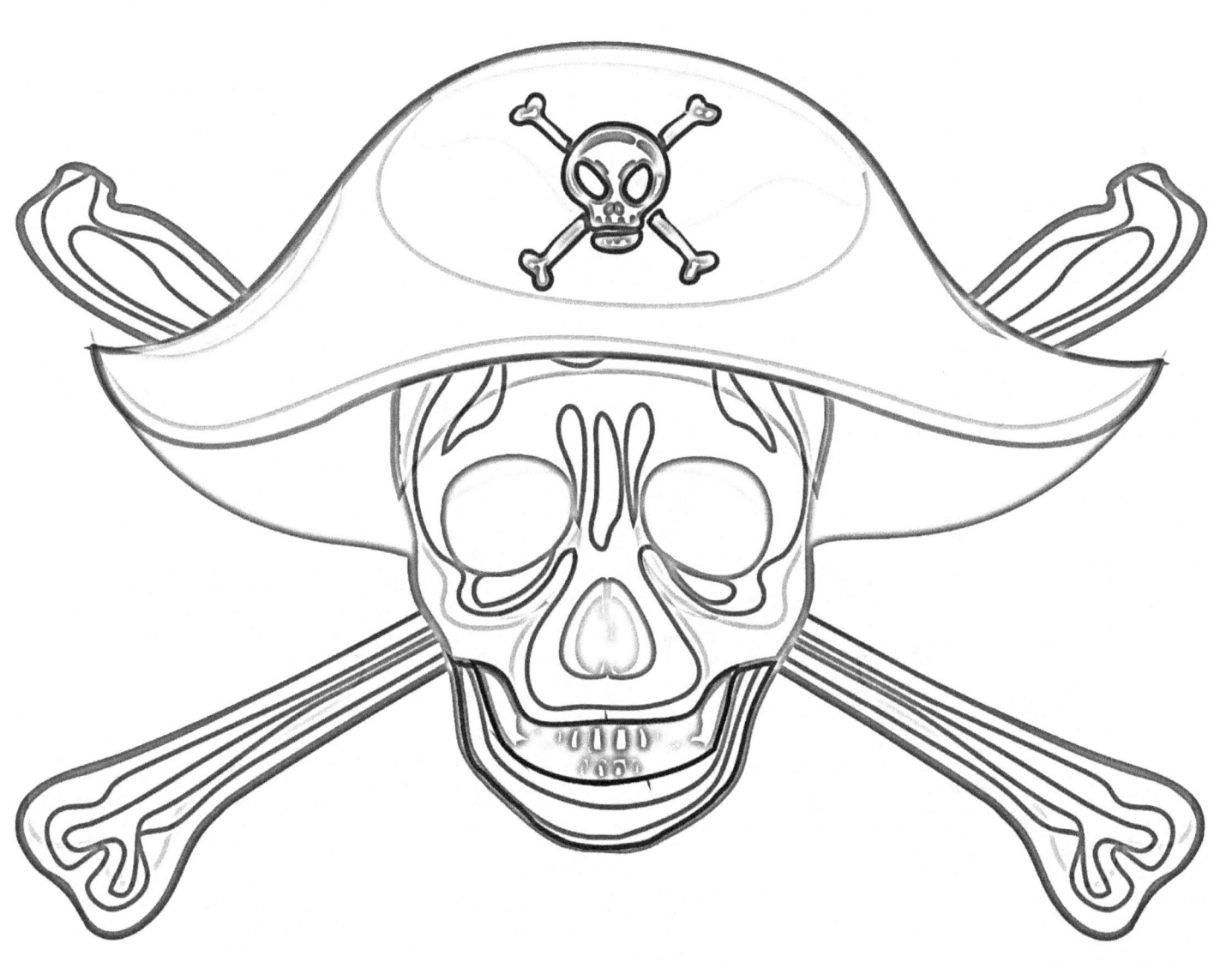

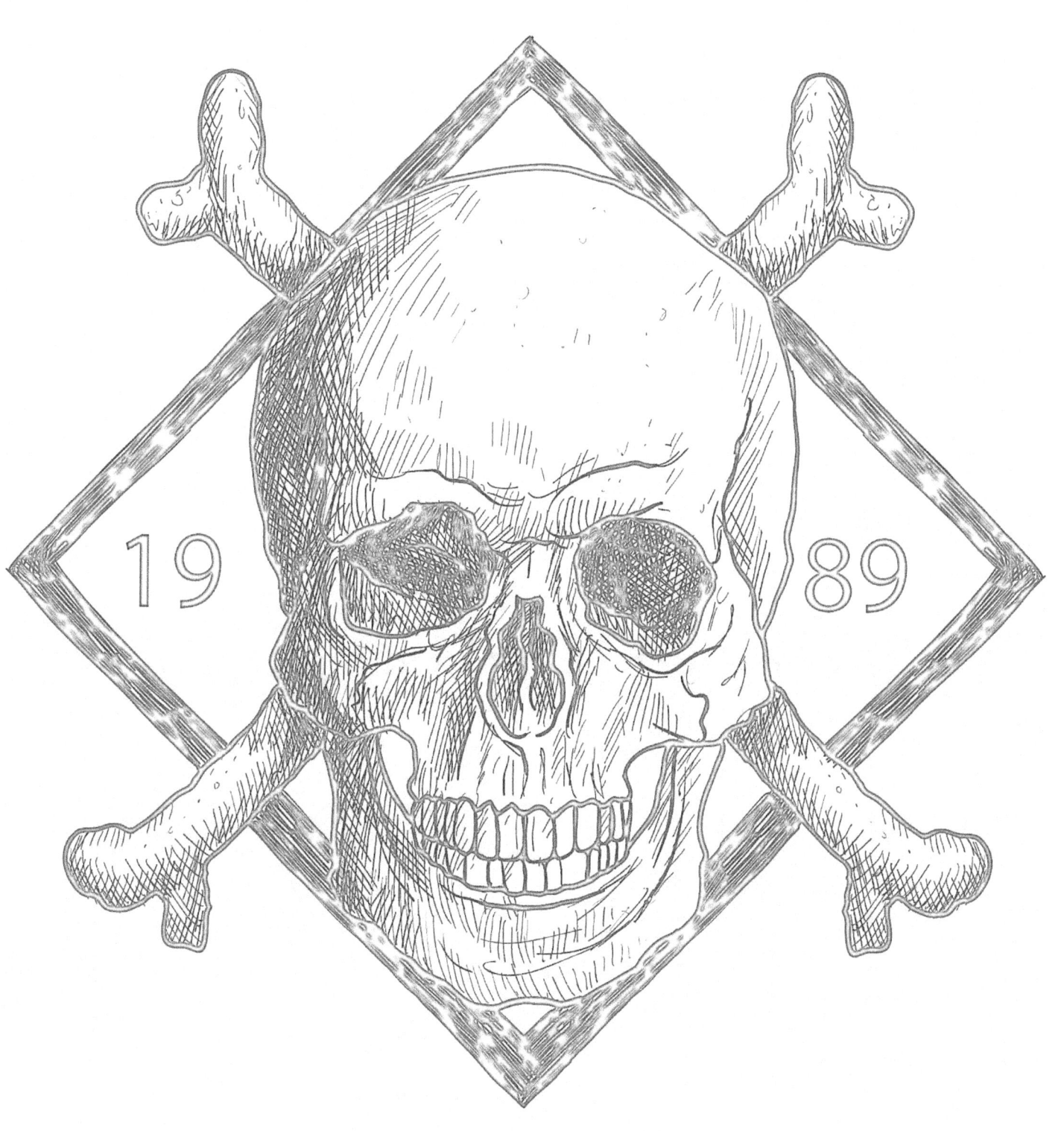

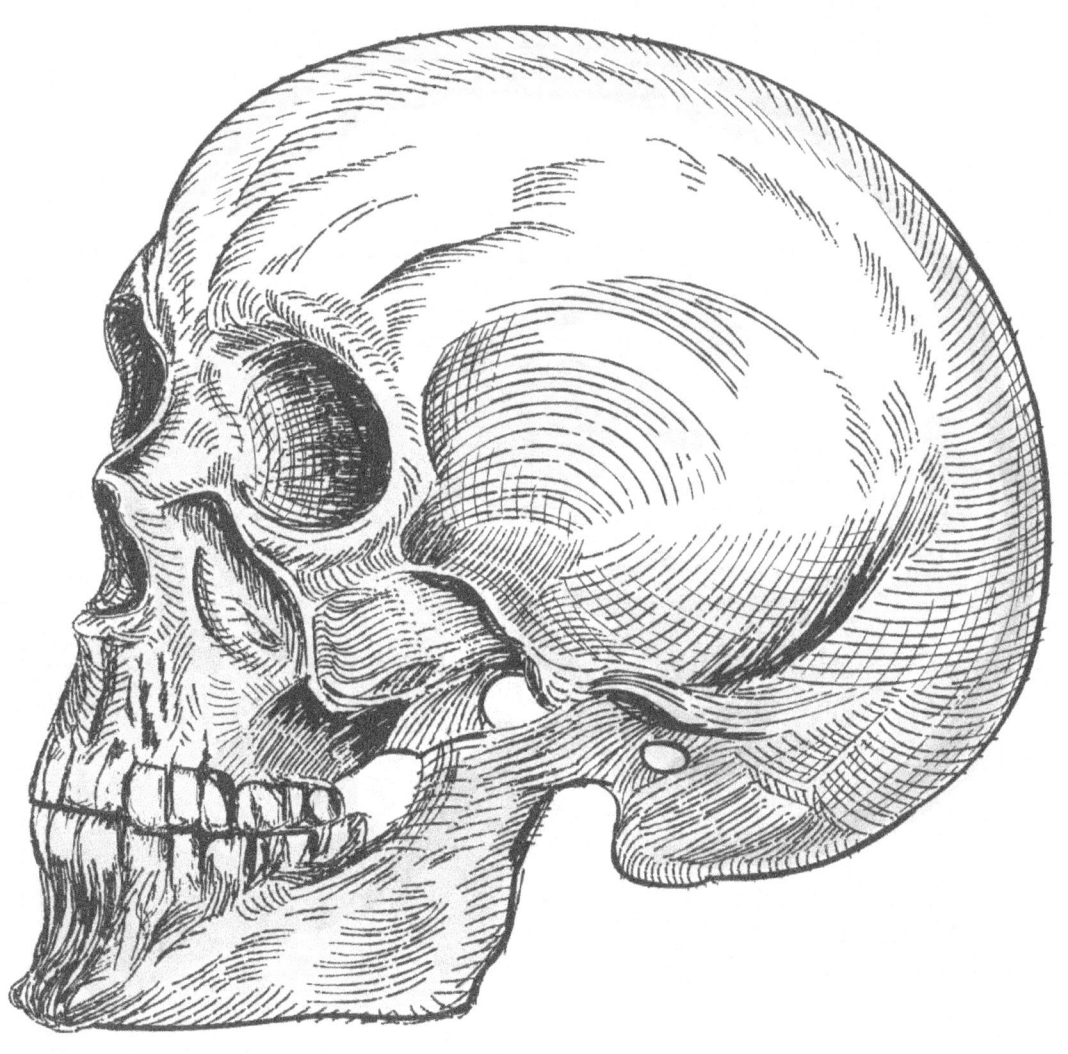

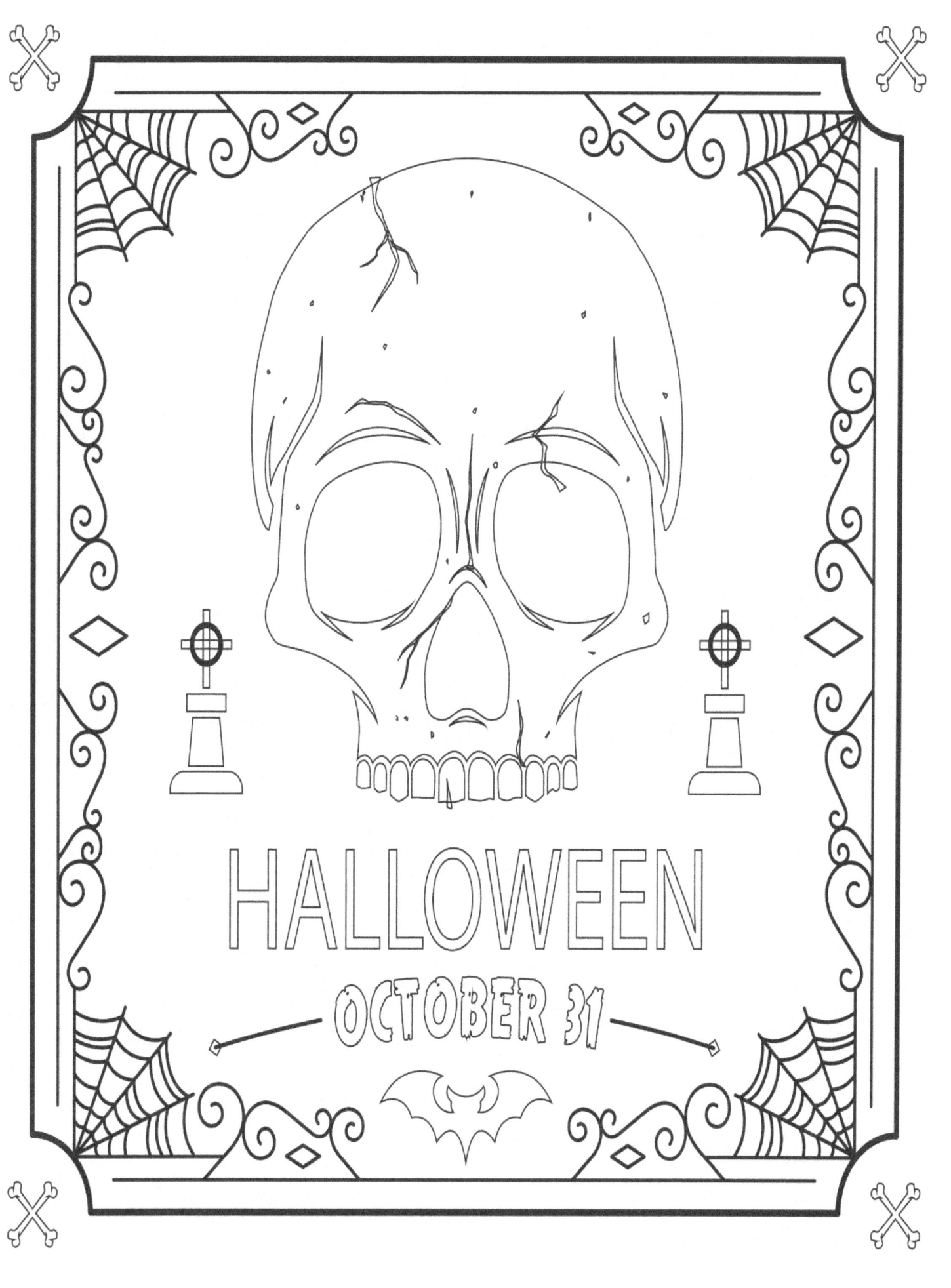

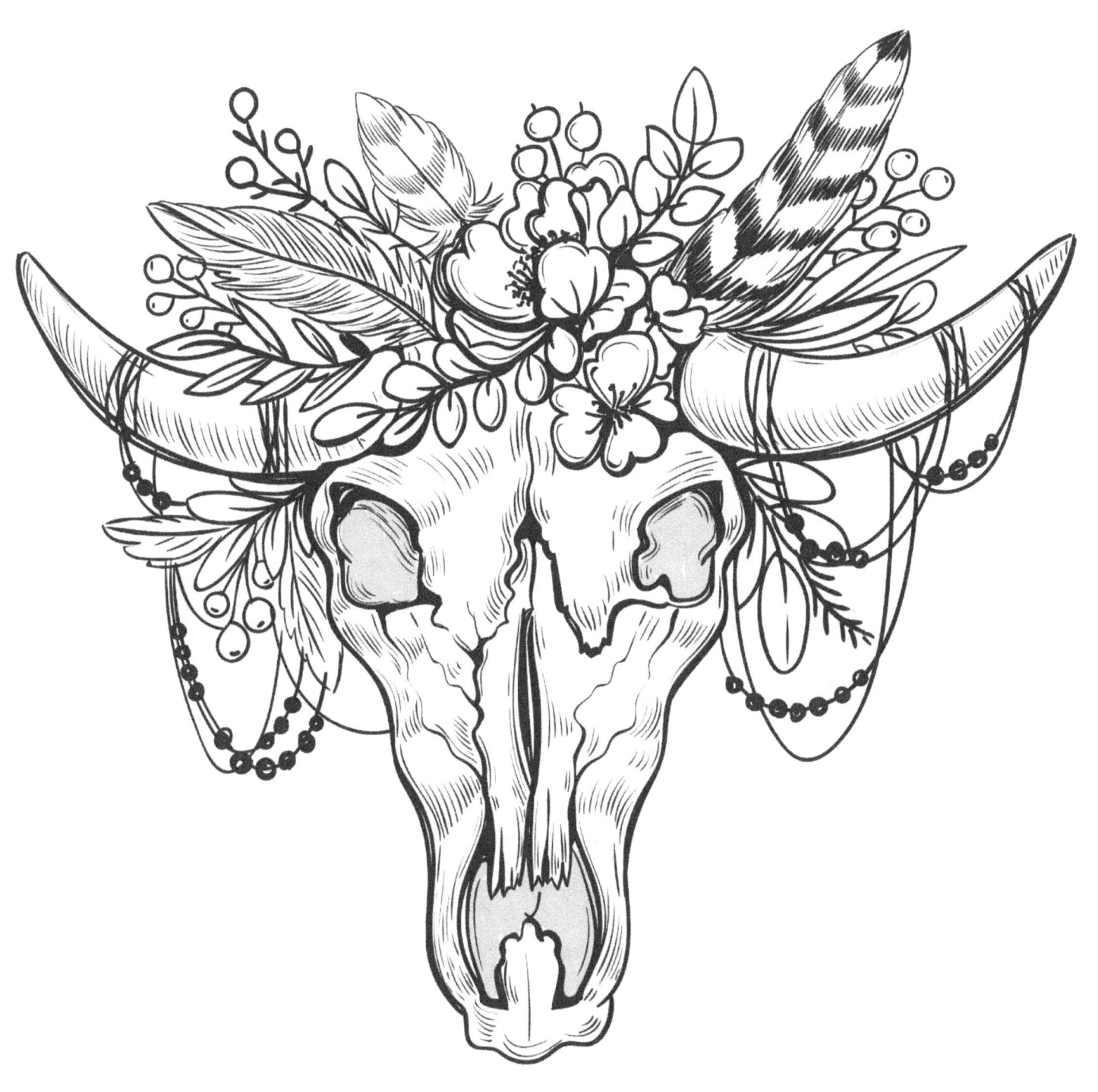

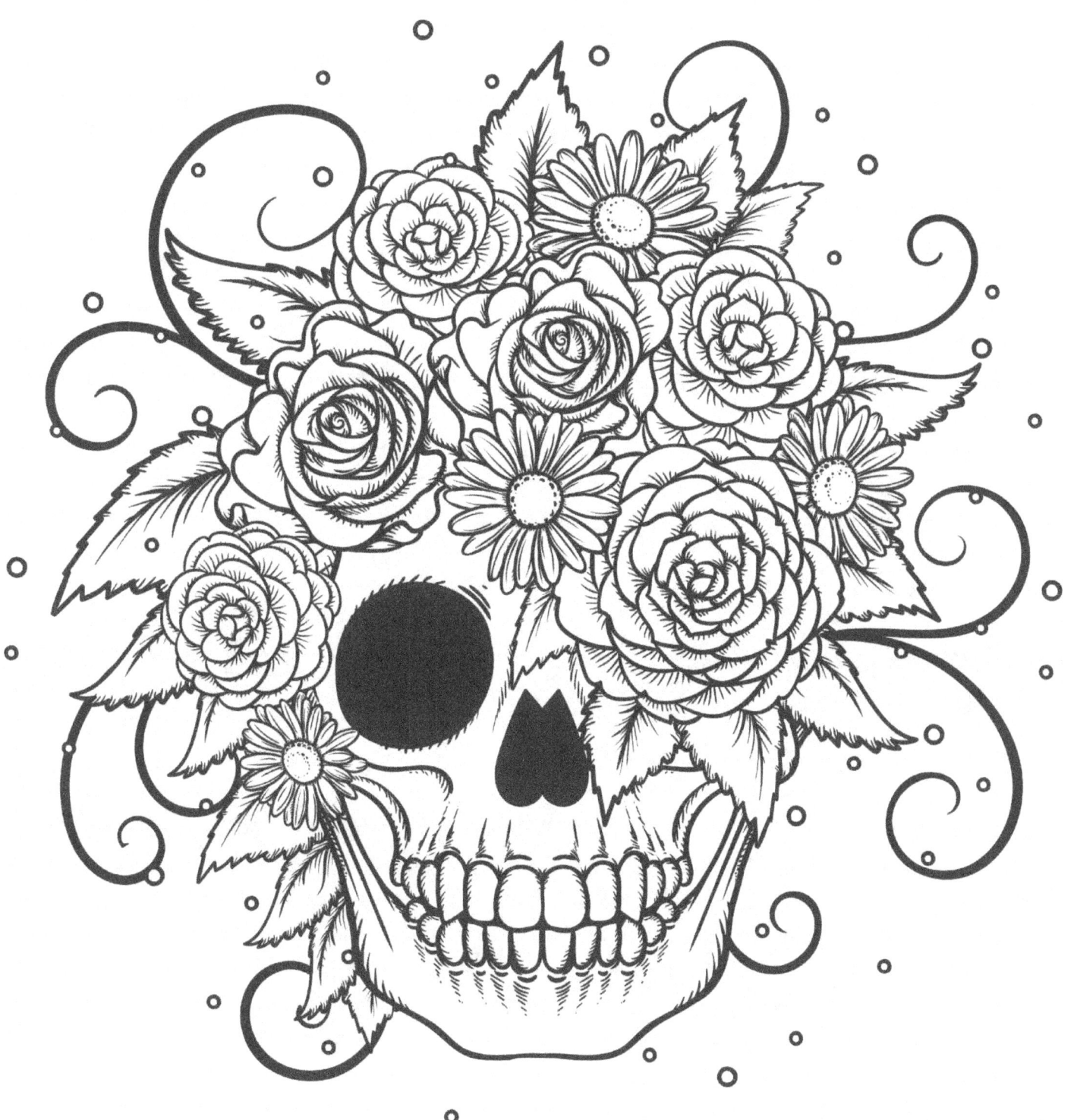

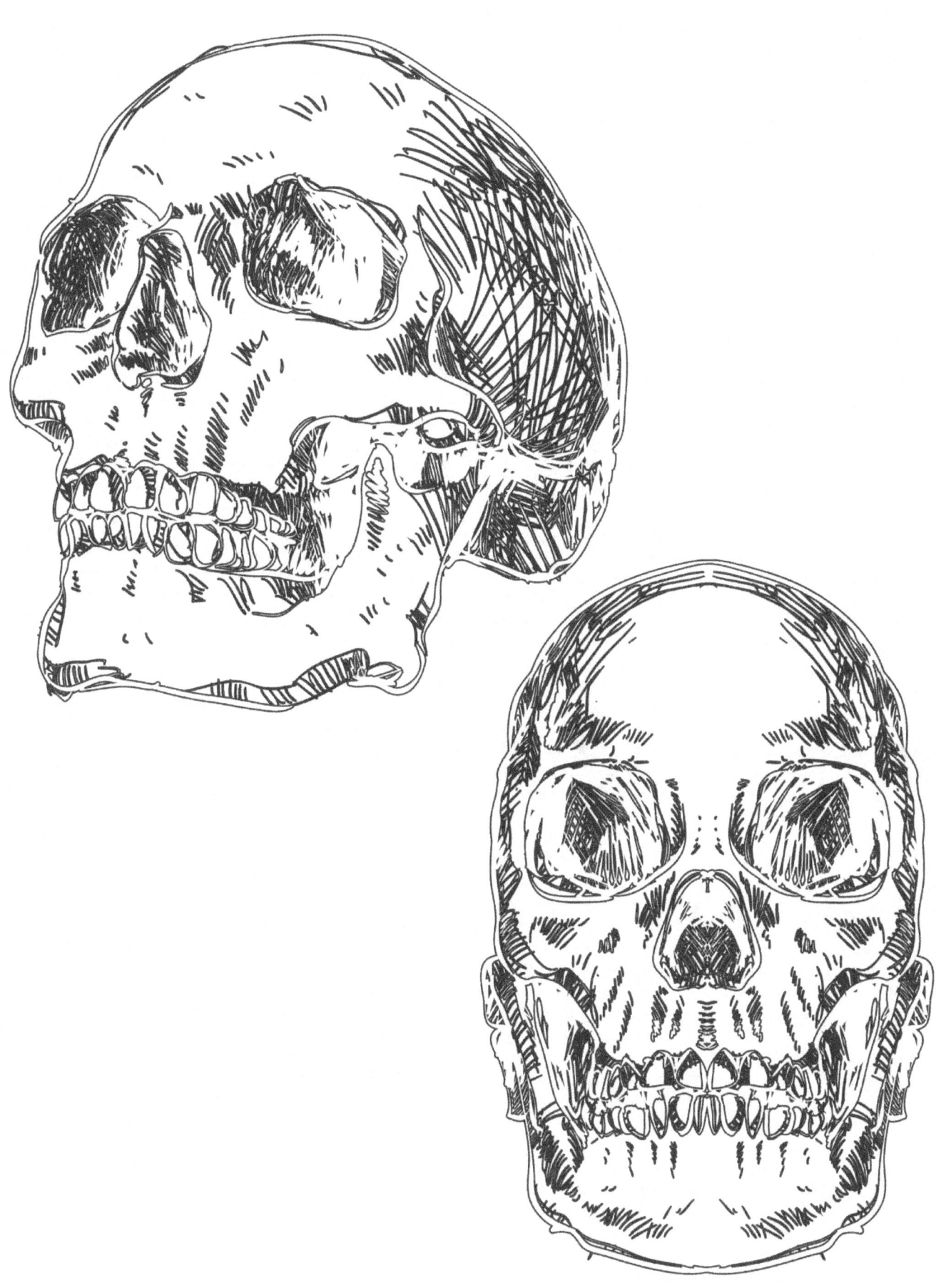

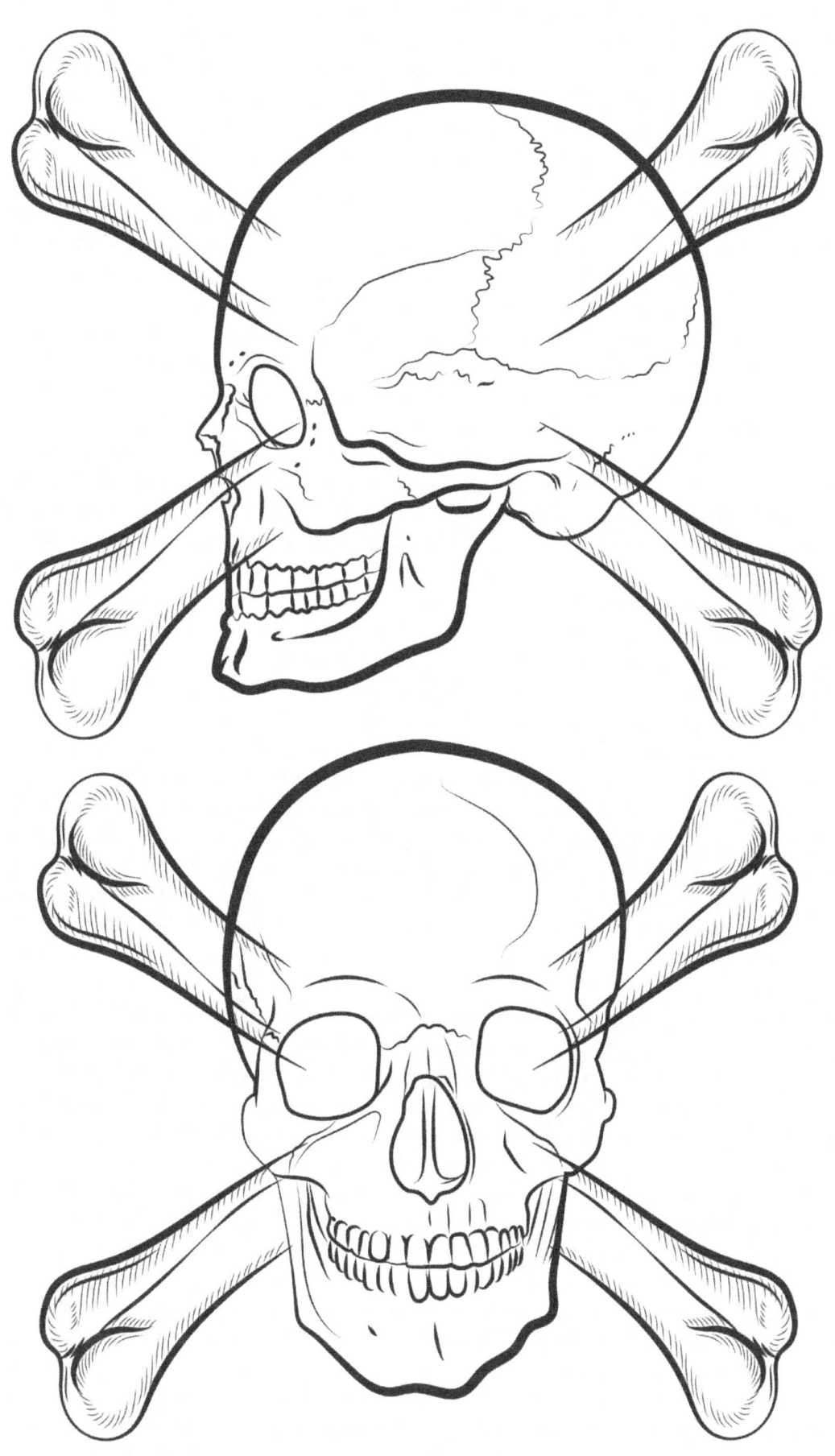

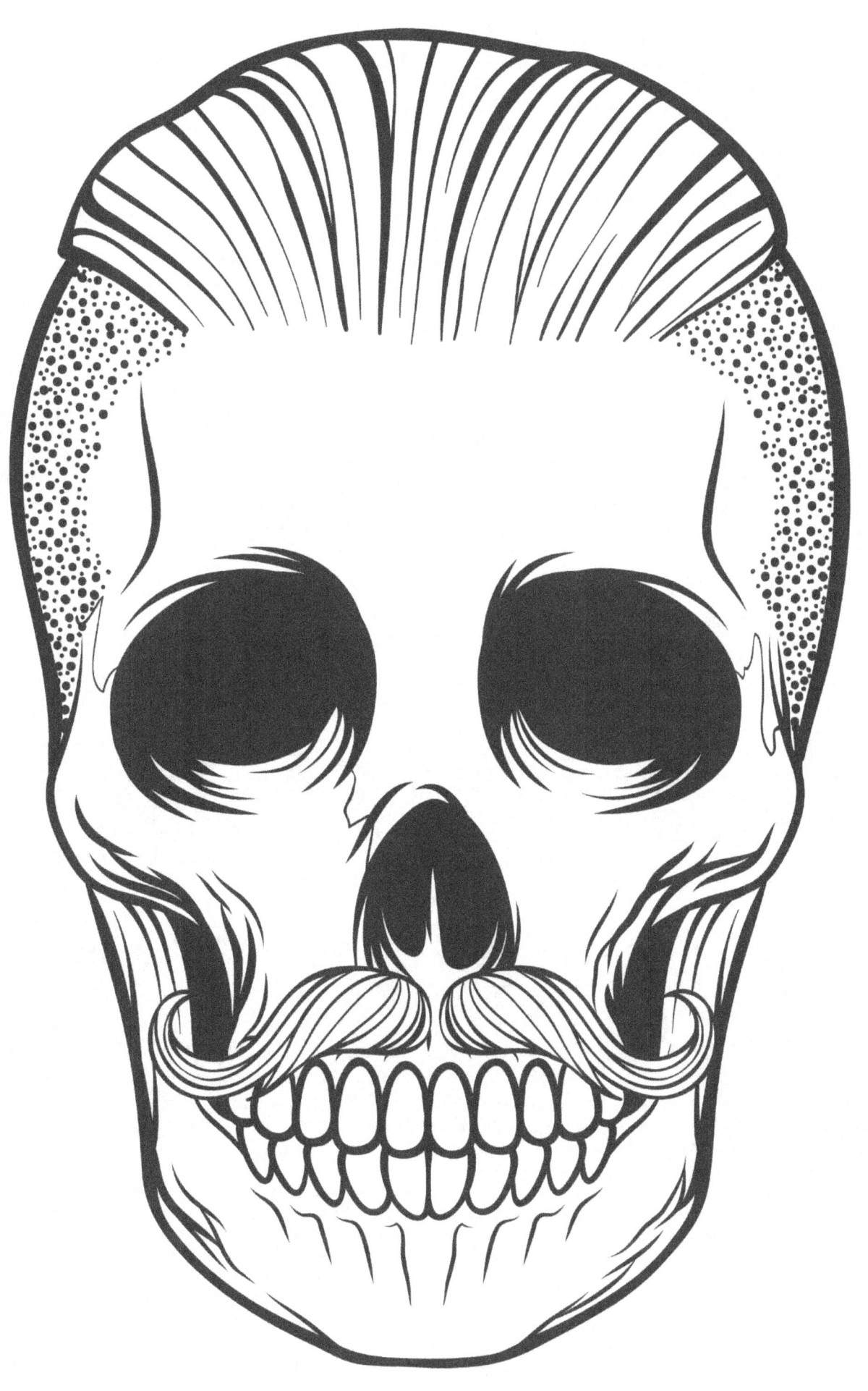

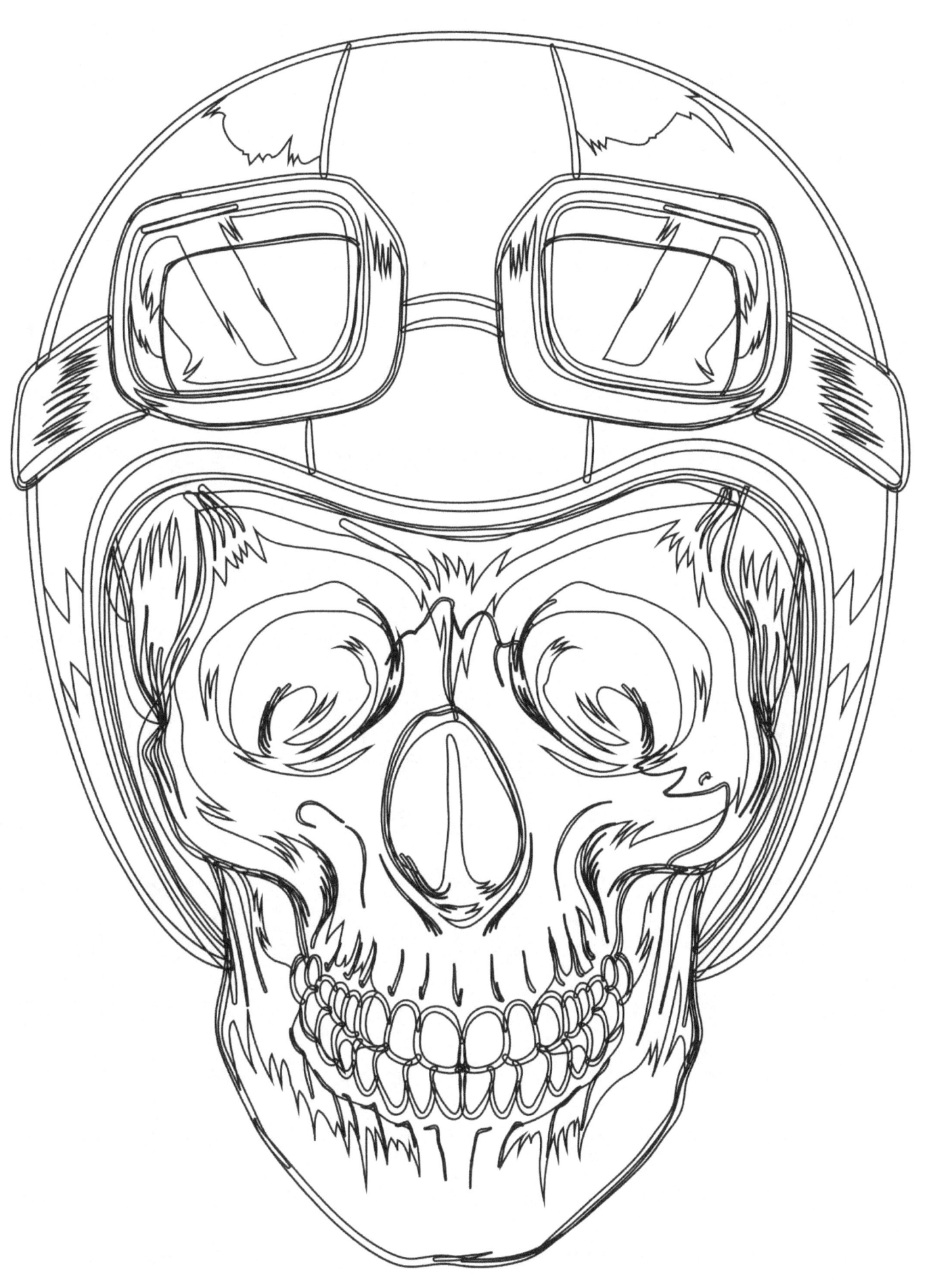

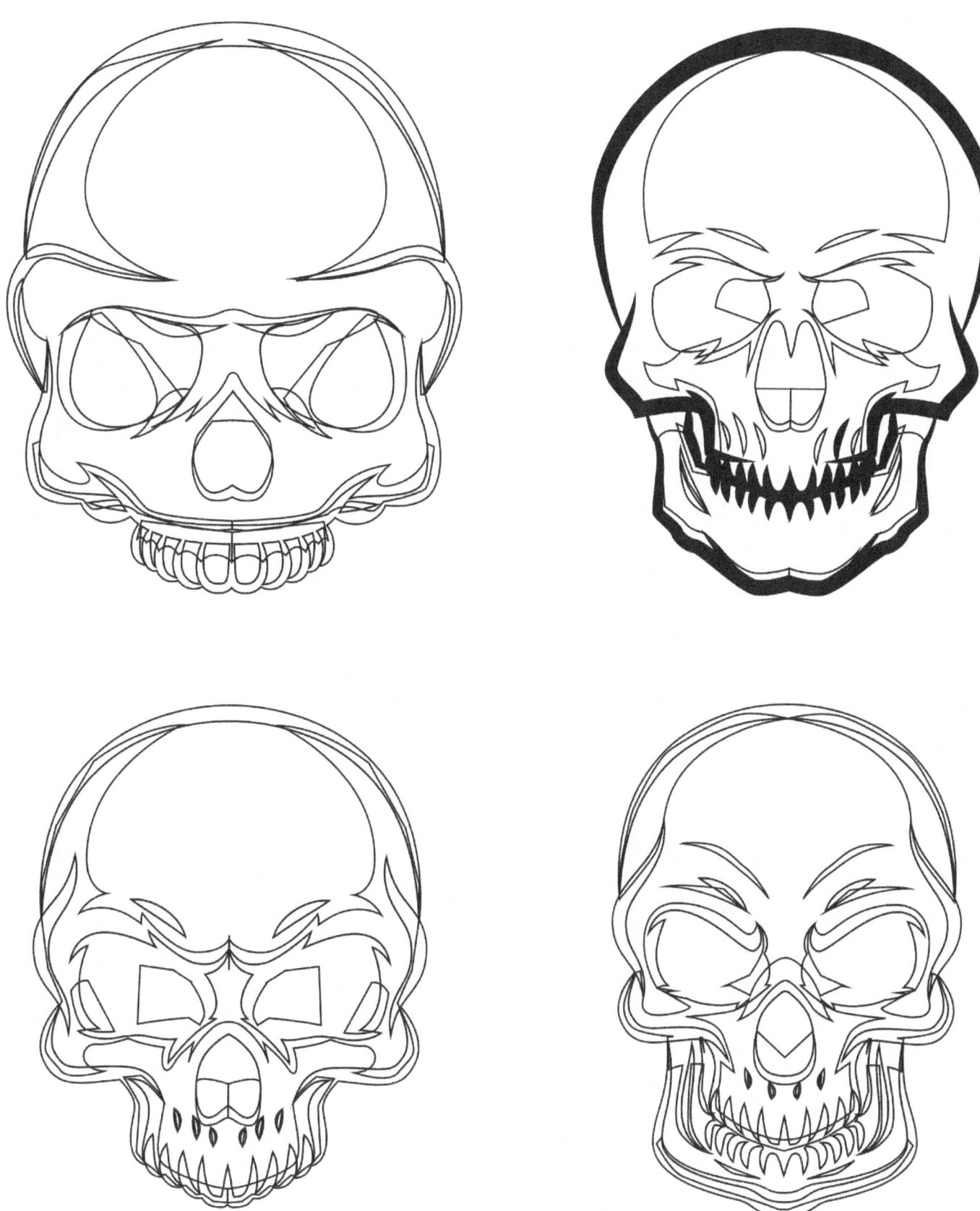

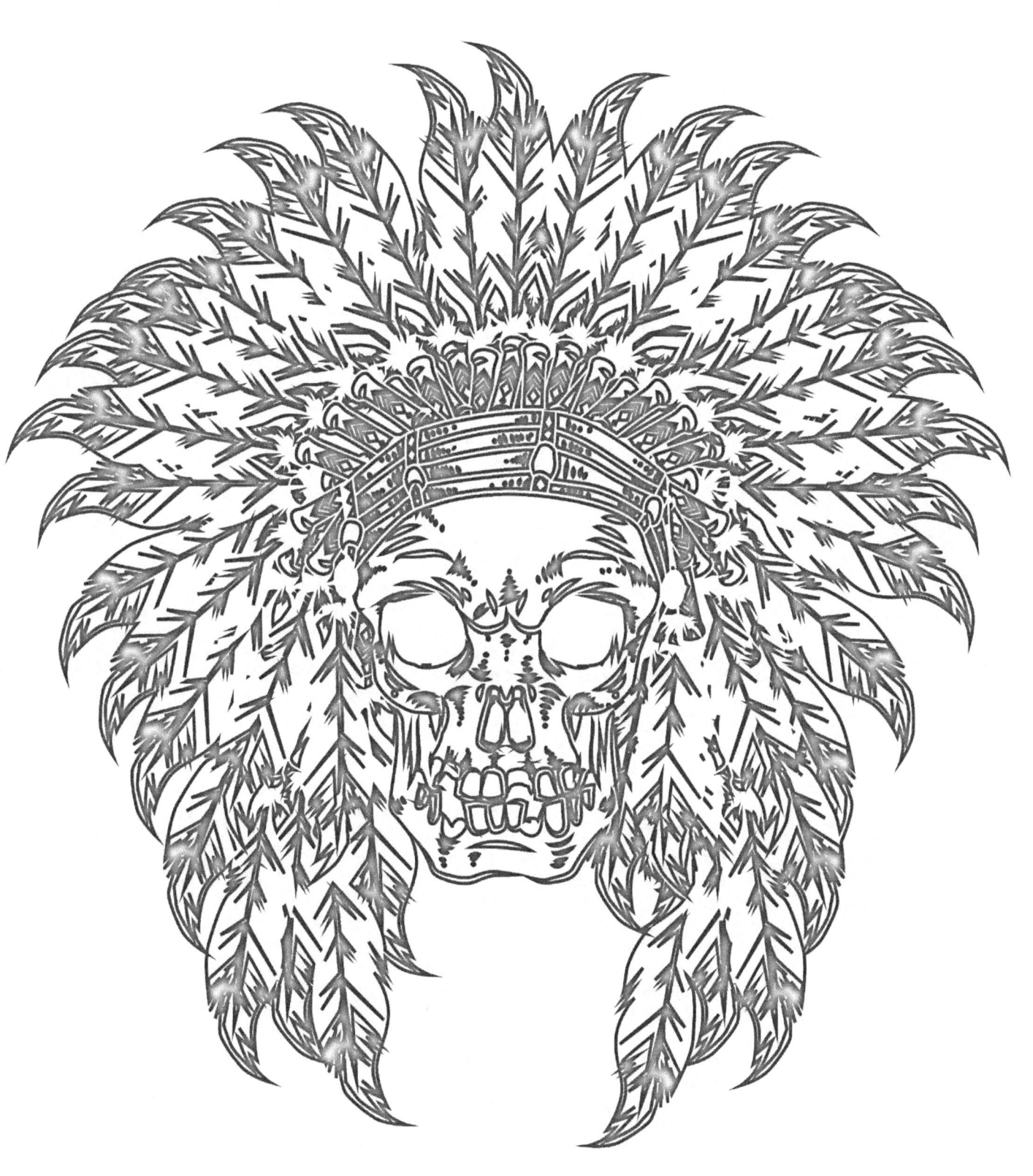

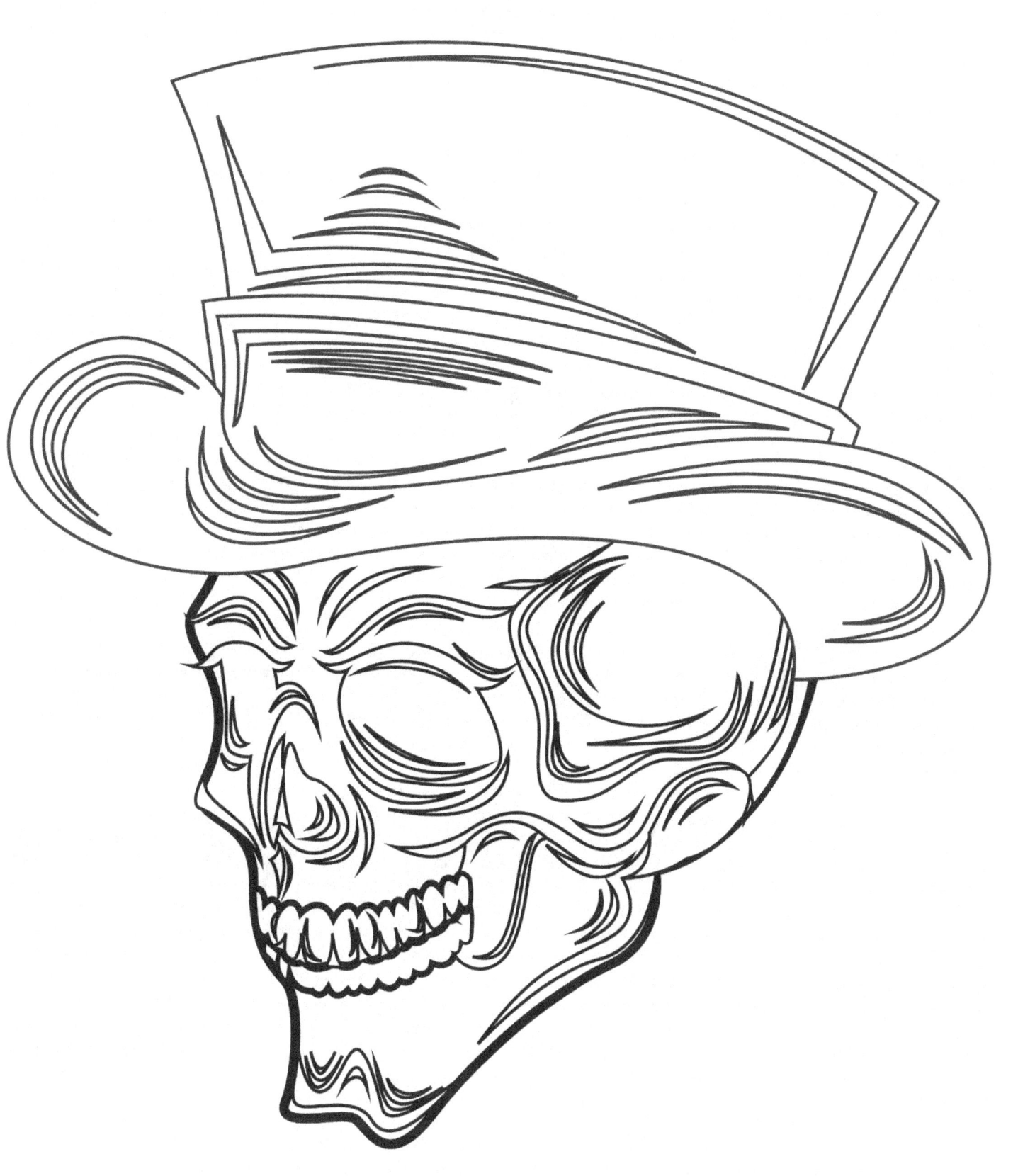

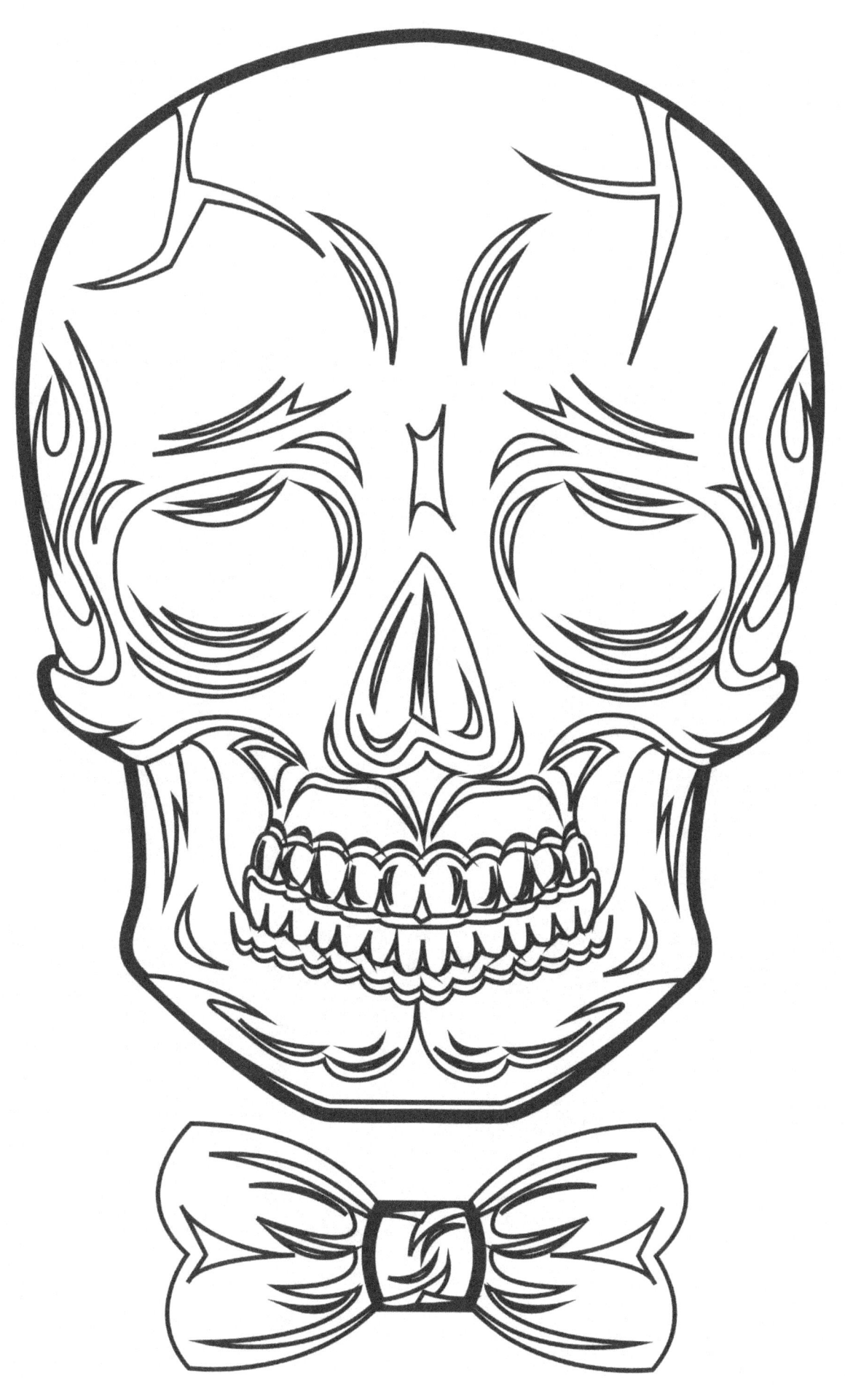

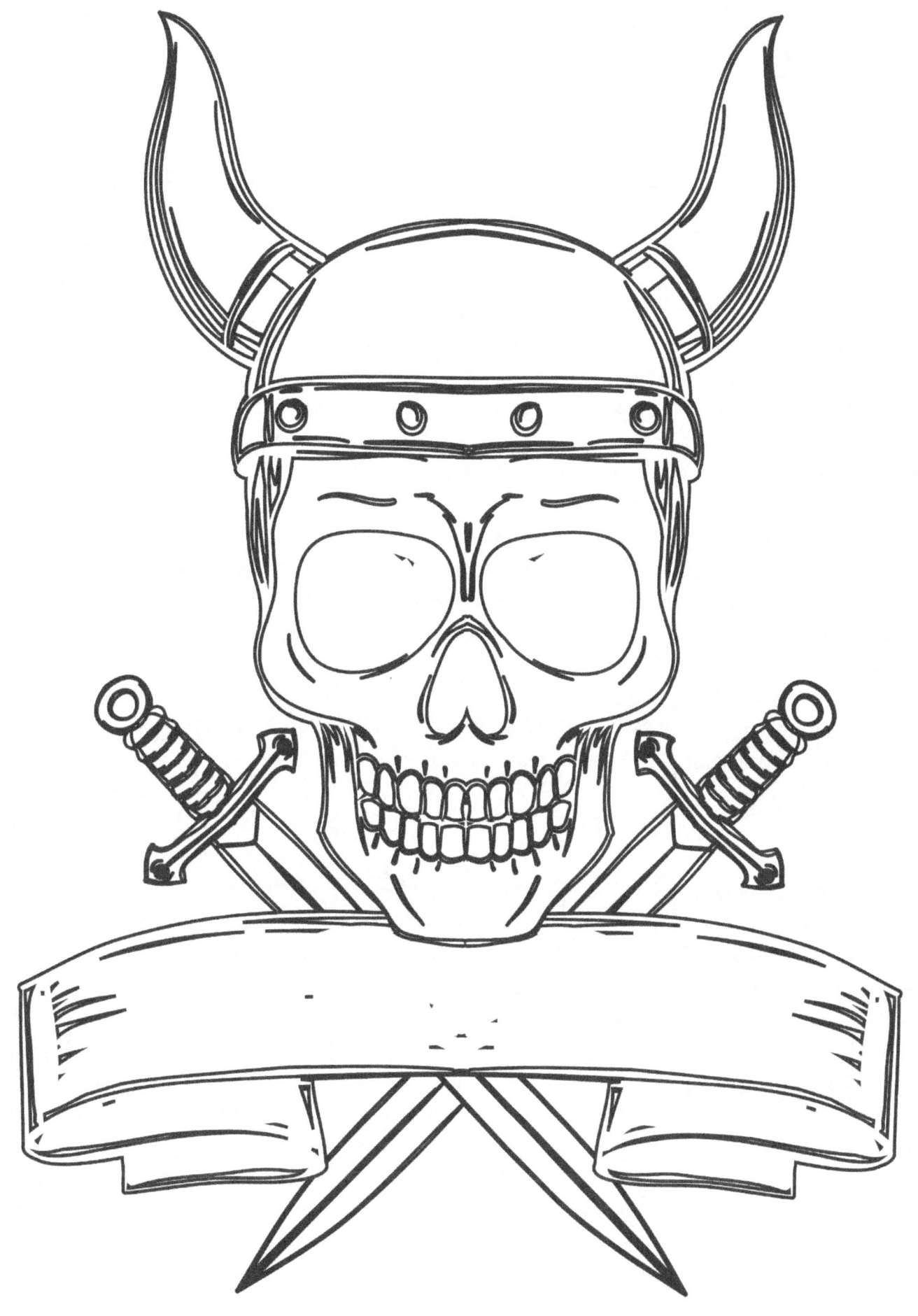

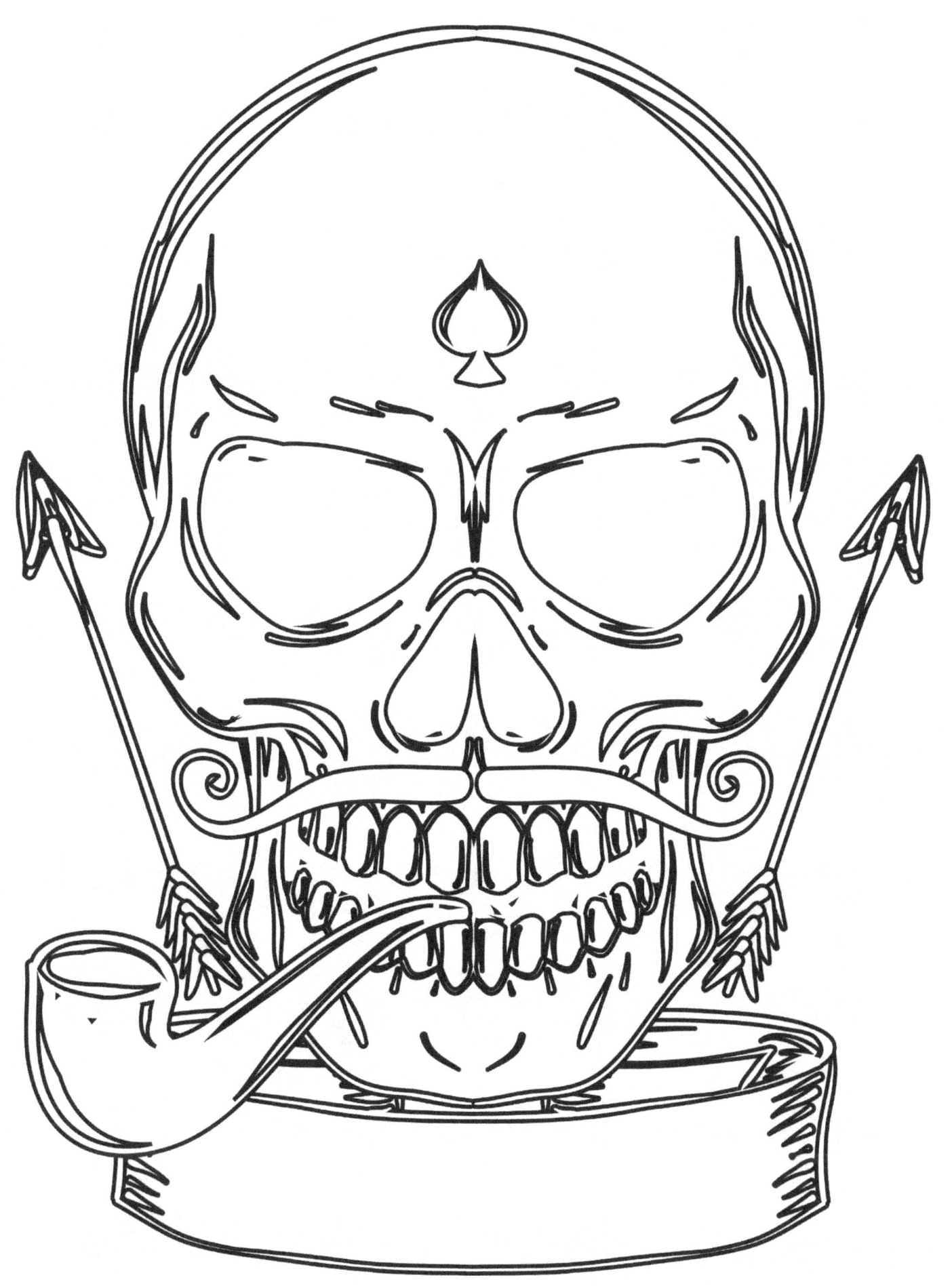

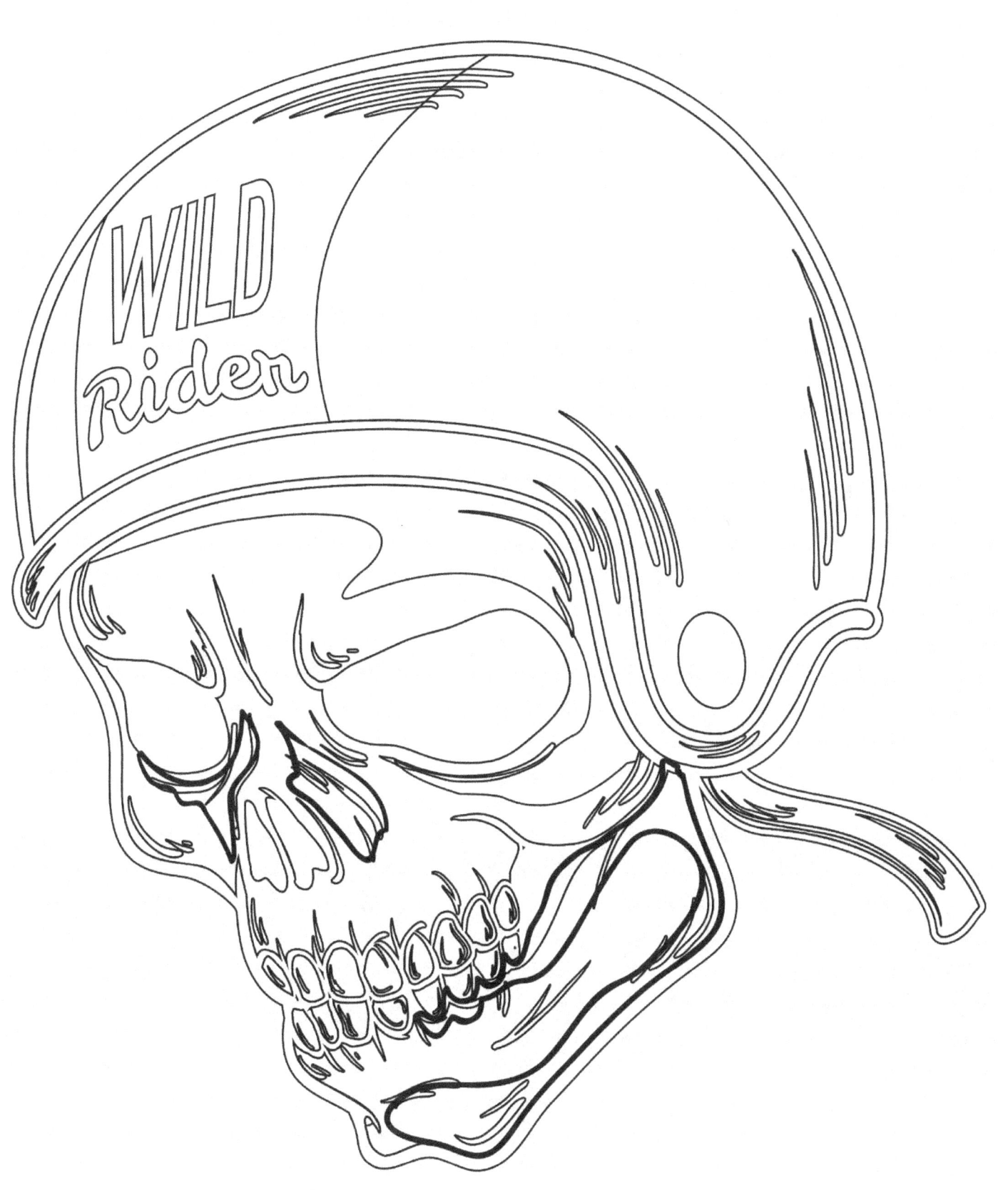

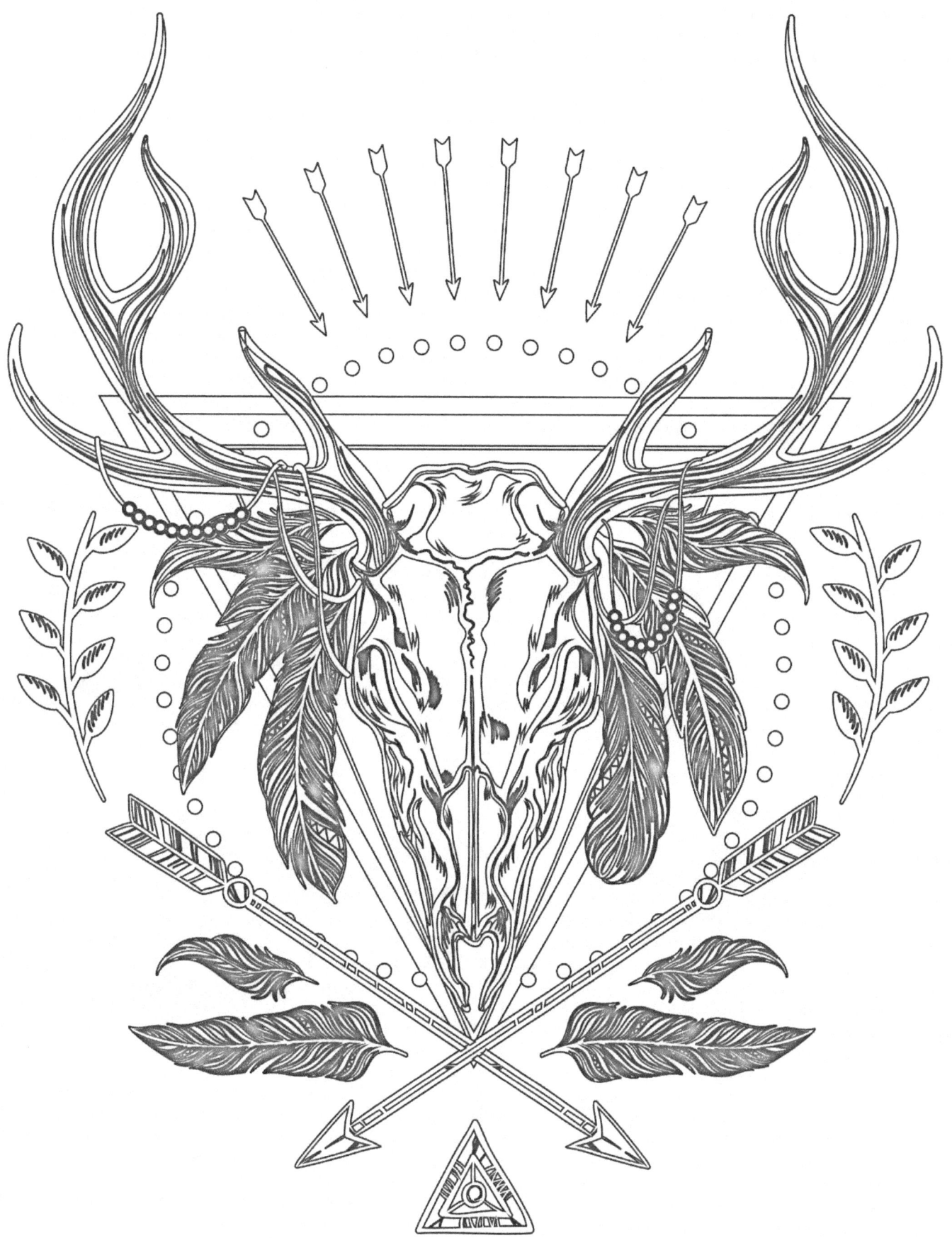

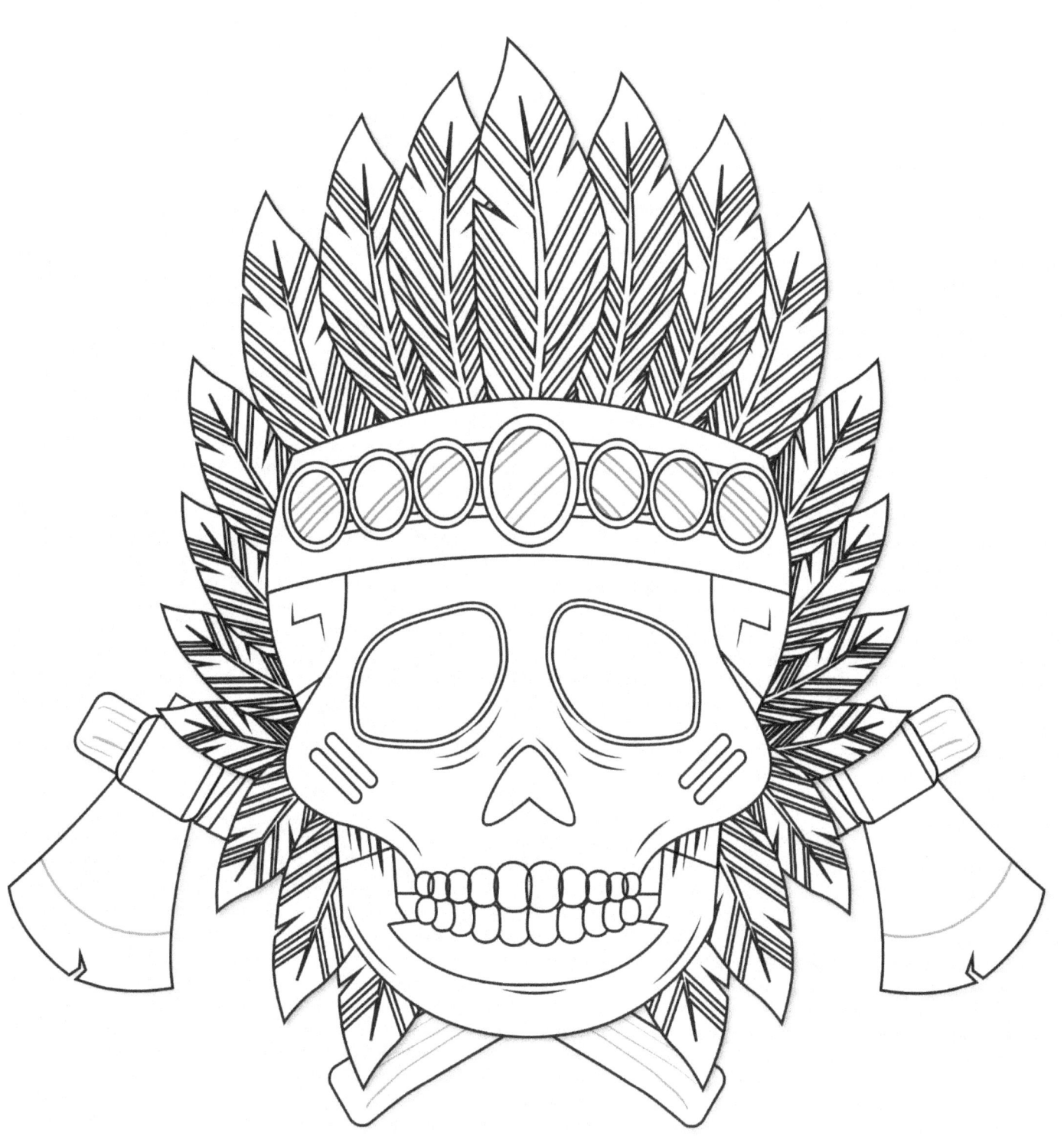

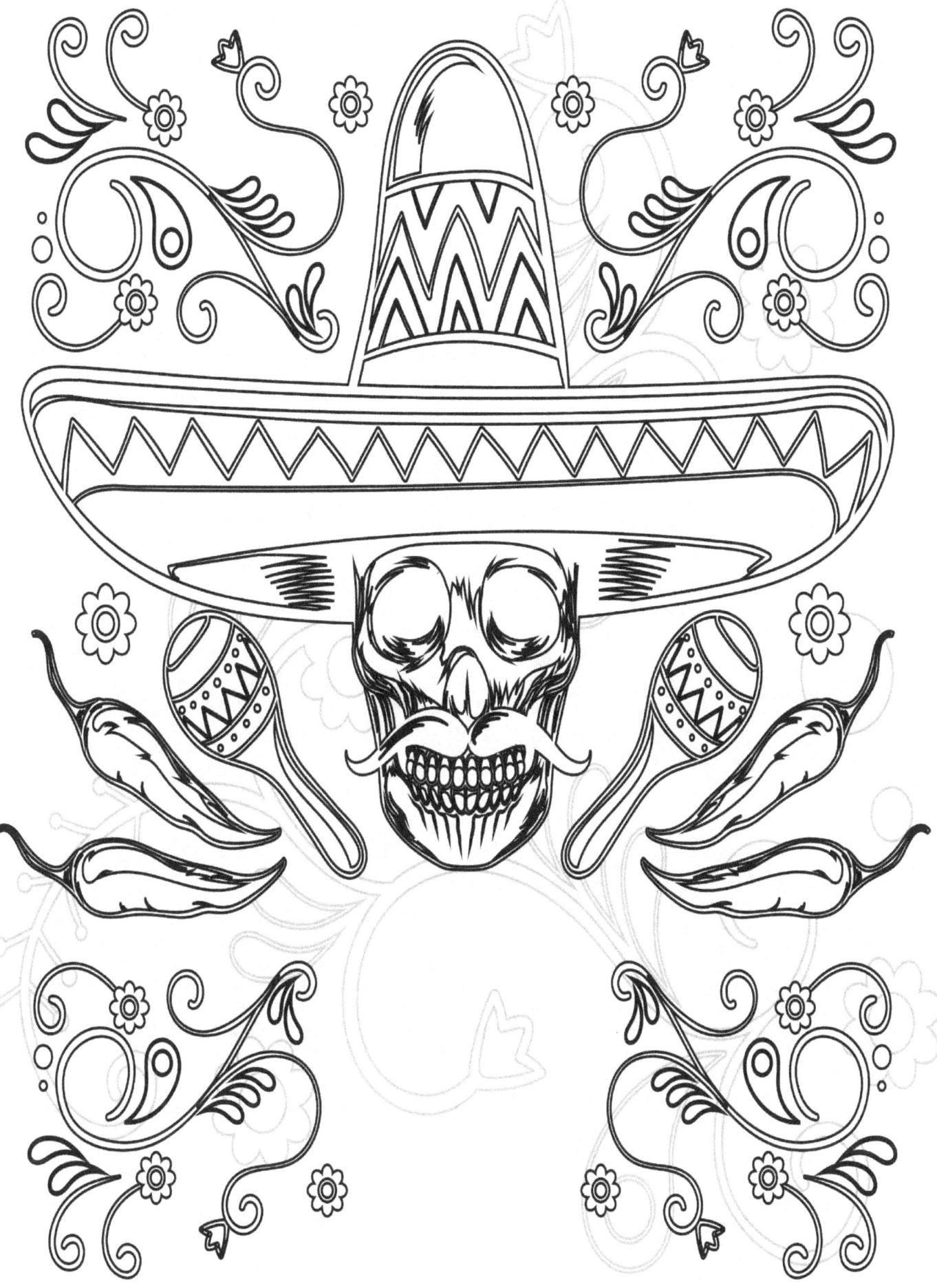

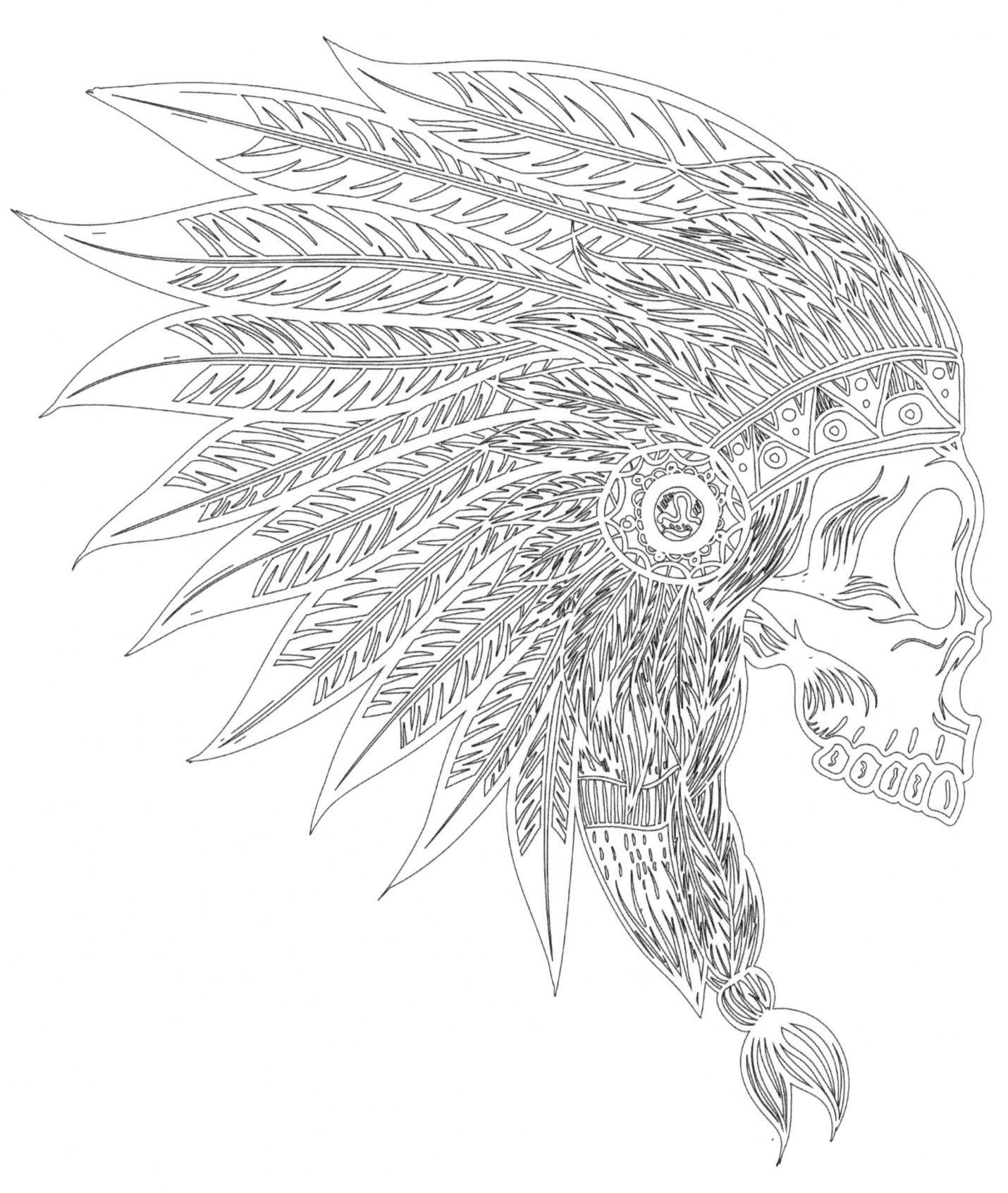

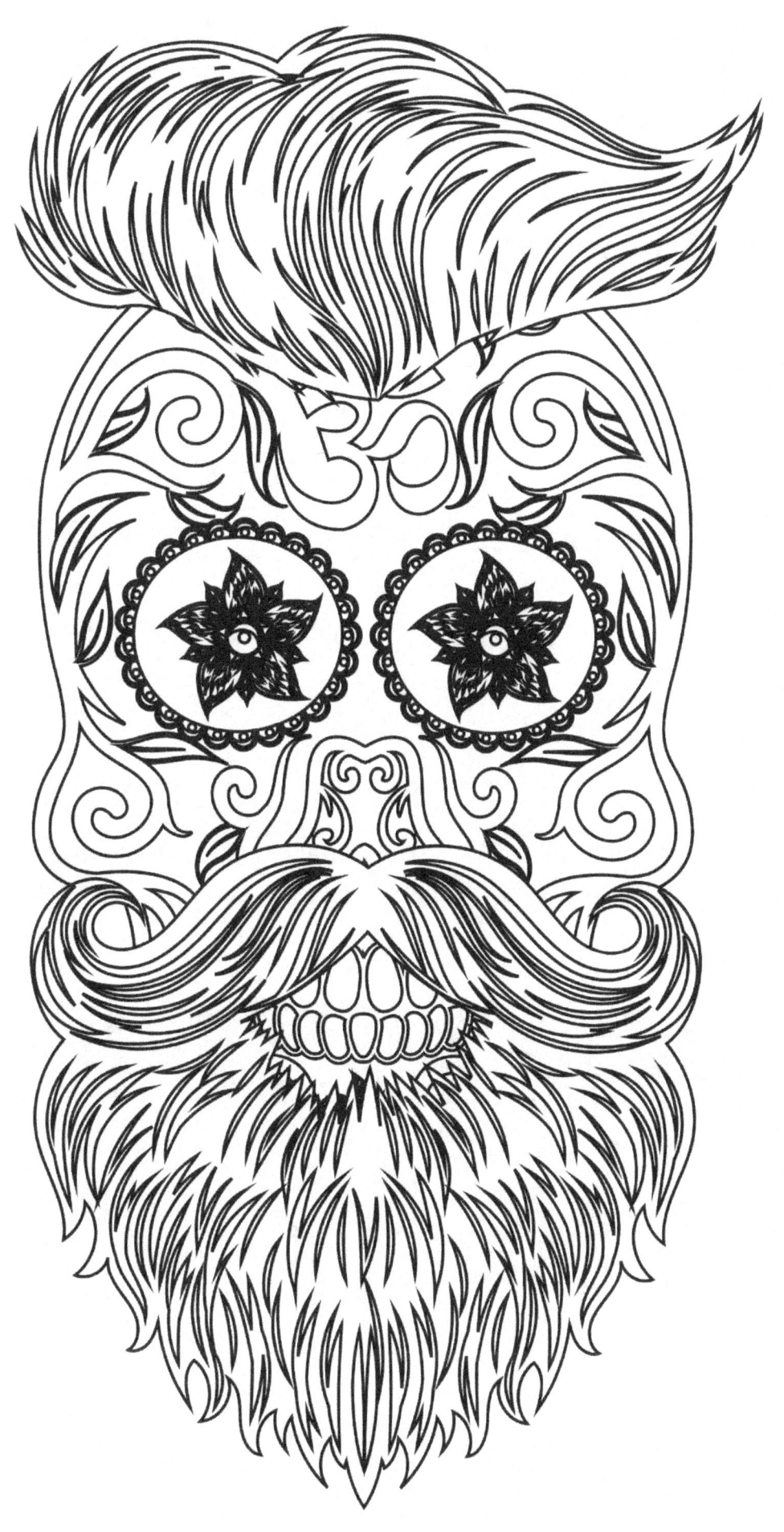

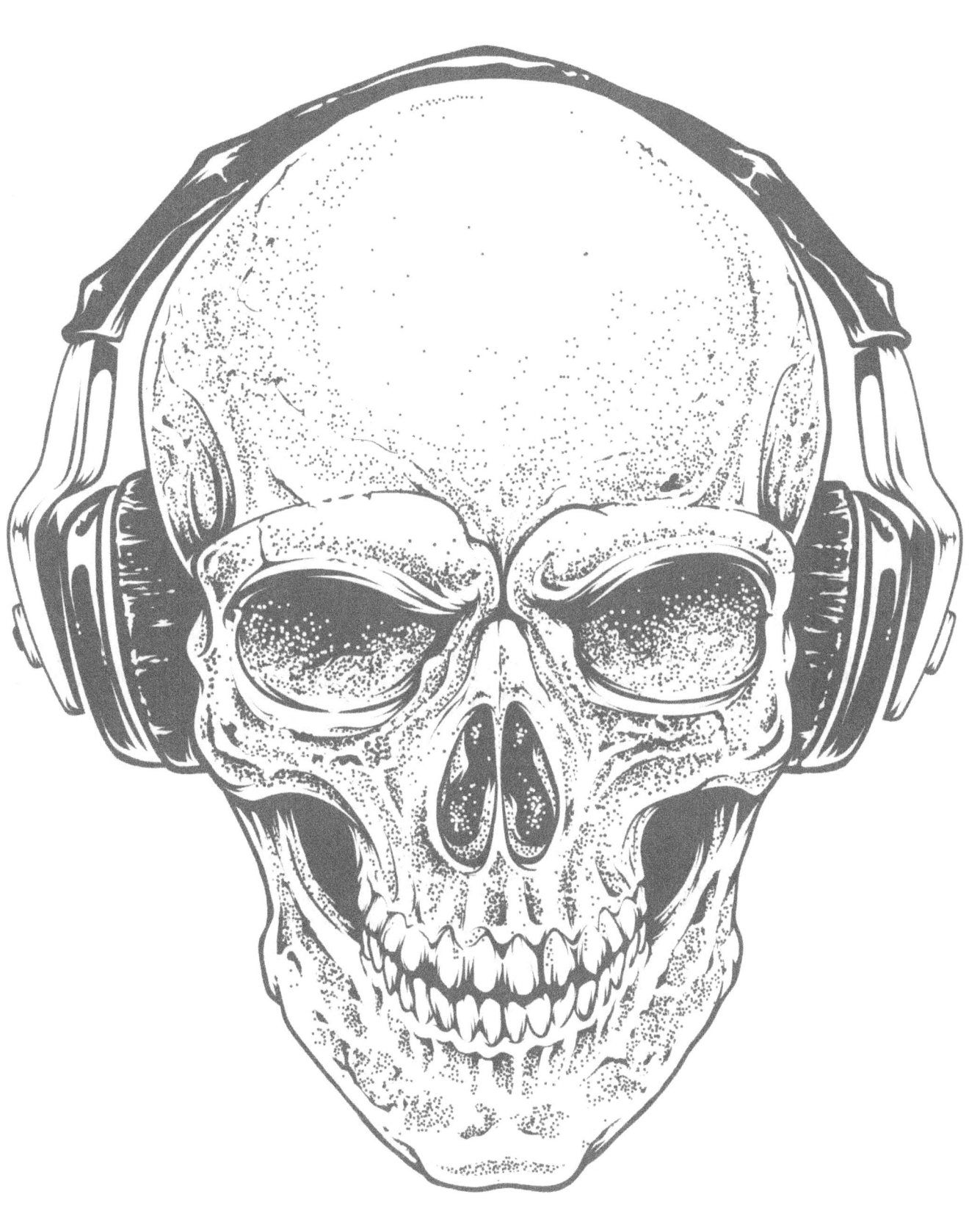

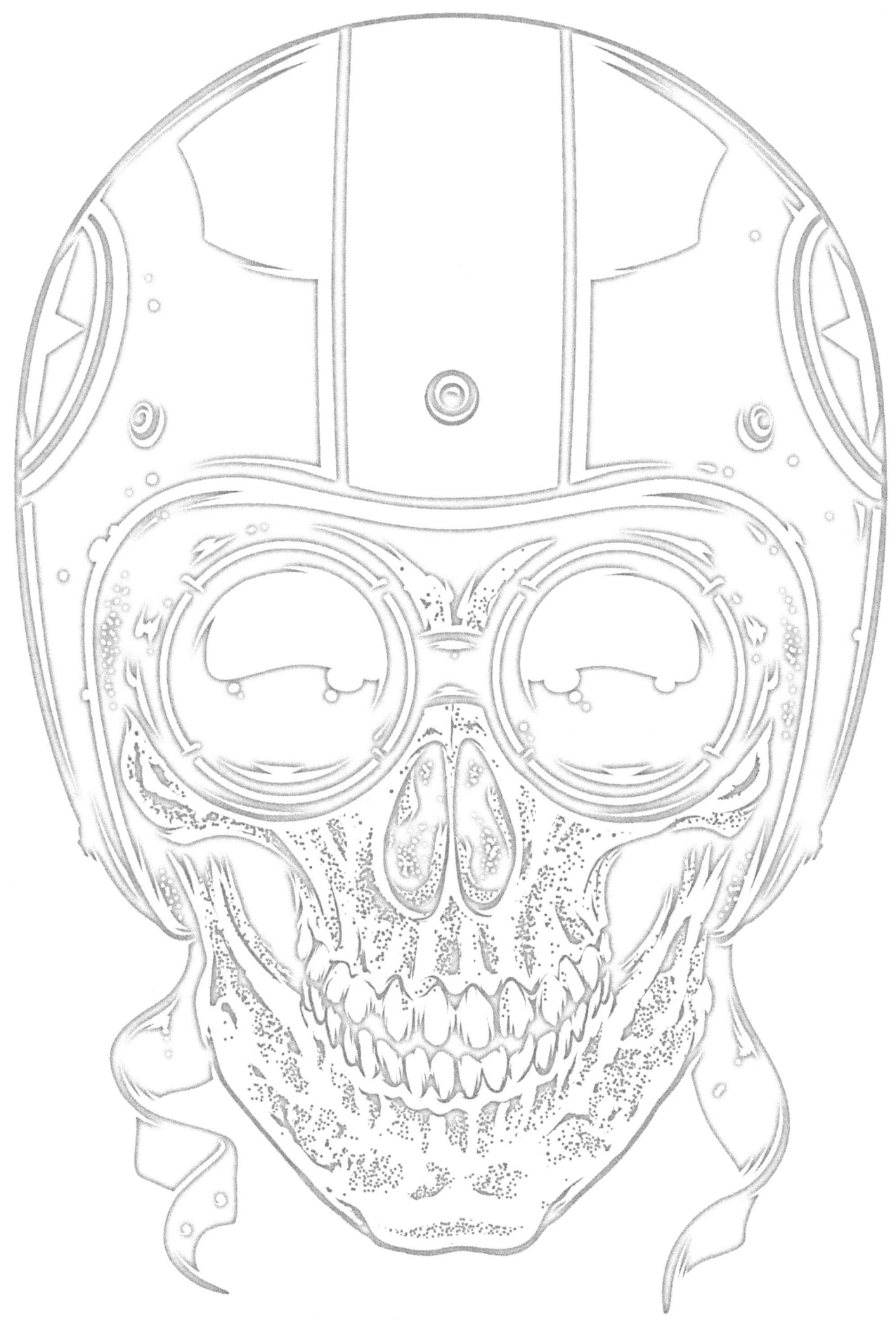

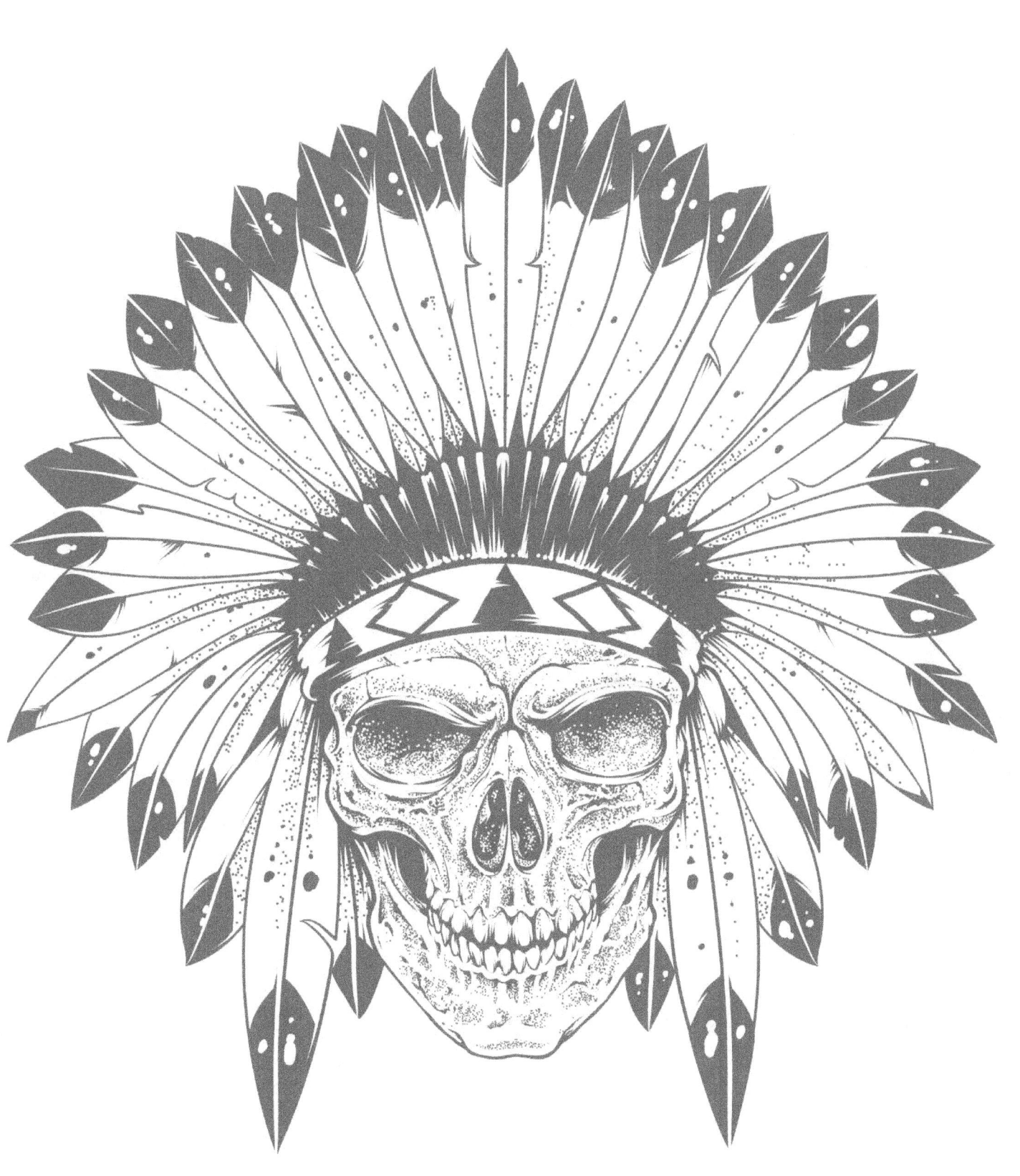

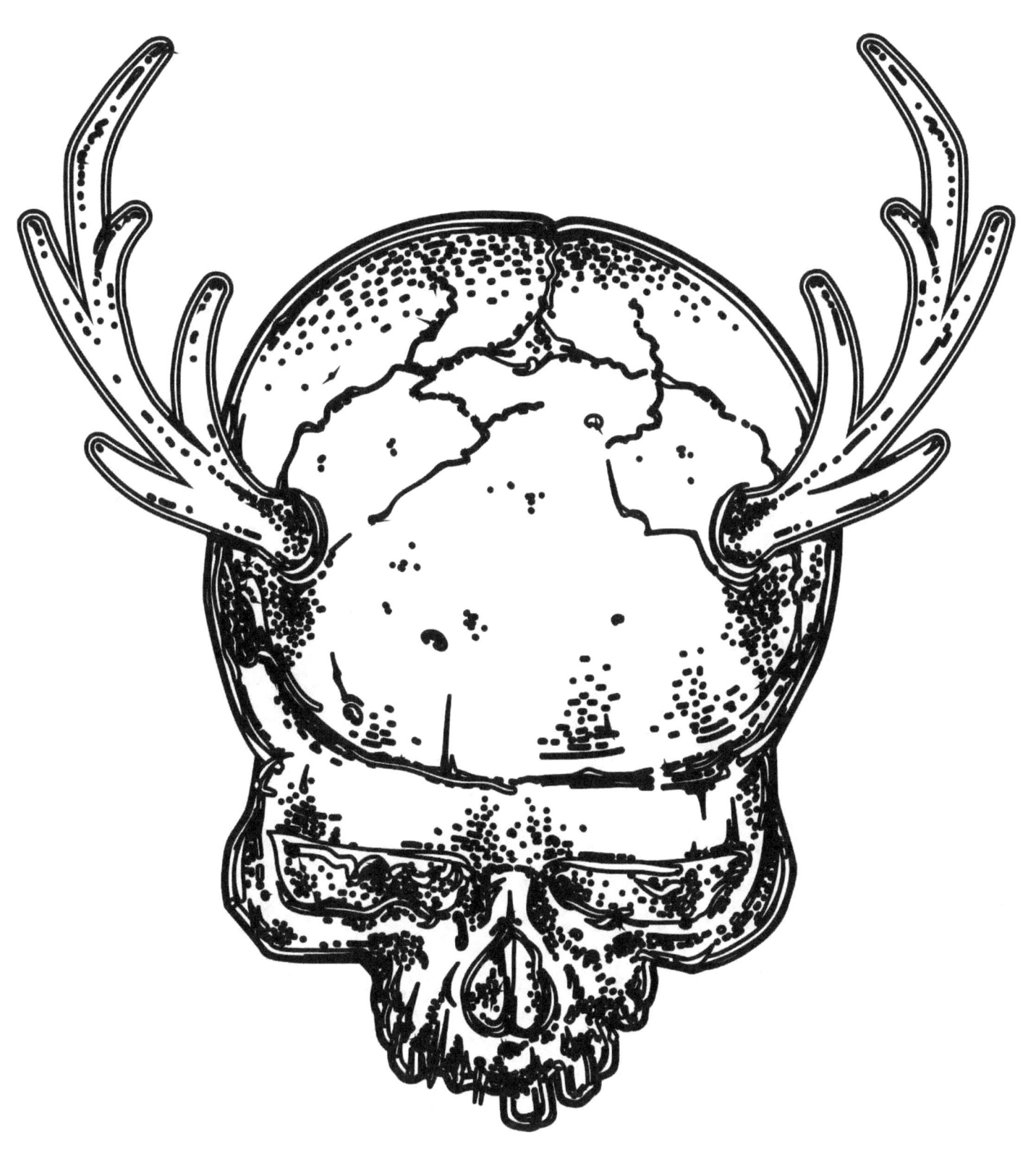

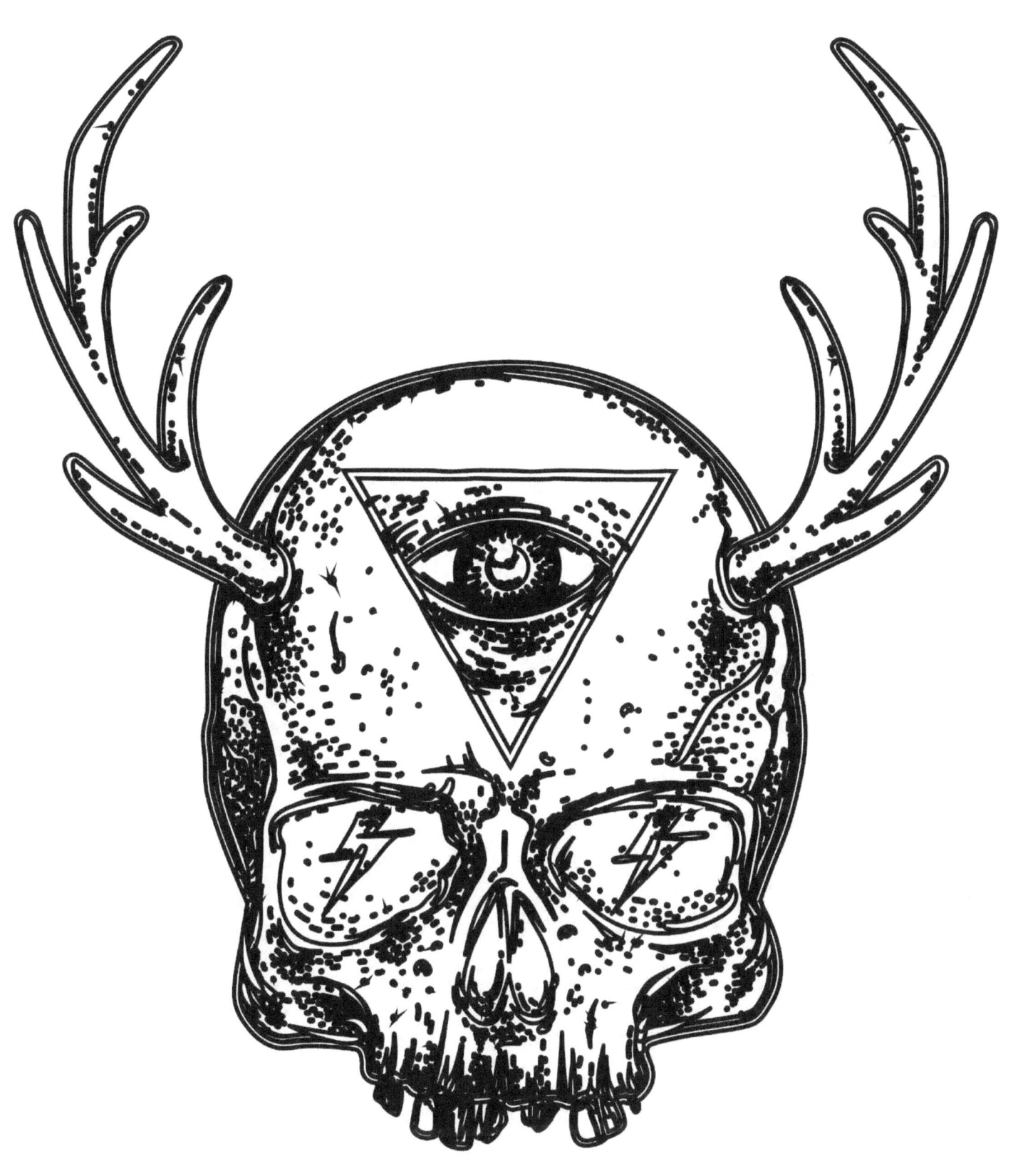

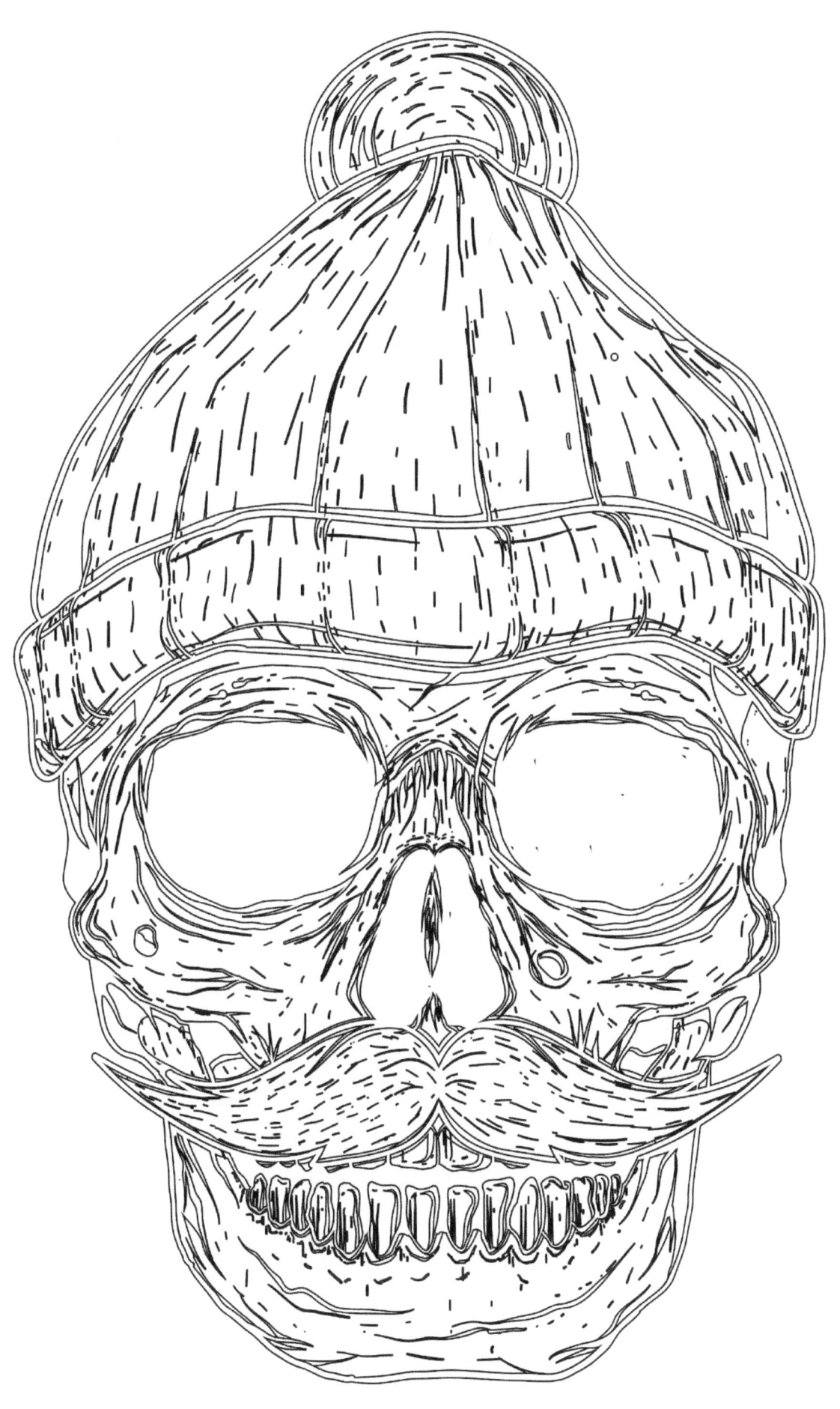

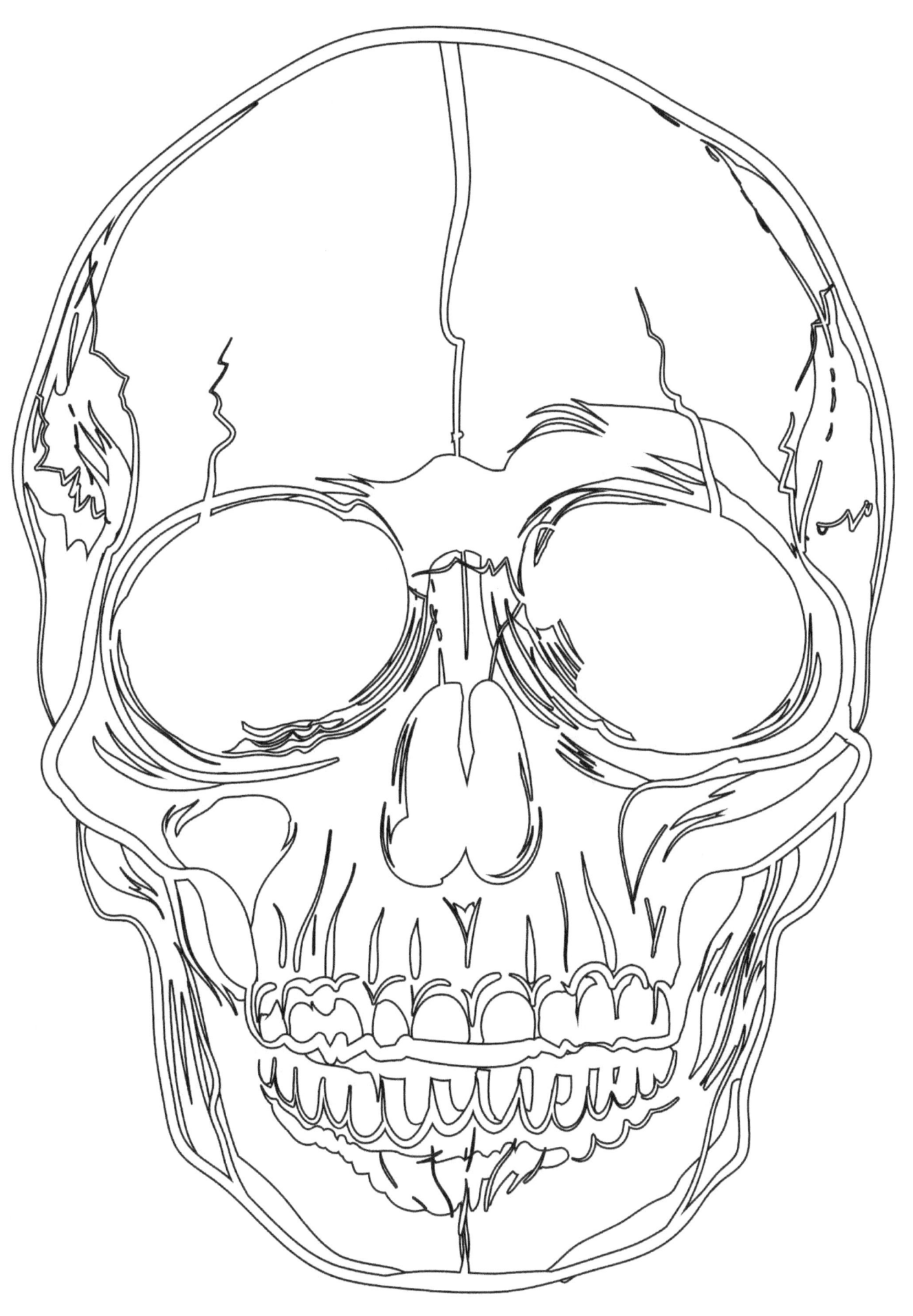

Thank you

Hope you've enjoyed your reading experience.

We here at FREEDOM BIRD DESIGN will always strive to deliver to you the highest quality guides.

So I'd like to thank you for supporting us and reading until the very end.

Before you go, would you mind leaving us a review on Amazon?

It will mean a lot to us and support us creating high quality guides for you in the future.

Thanks once again and here's where you can leave a review.

Get Free Ebook Coloring Page below

https://www.facebook.com/groups/1523056898003358/

Warmly yours,

FREEDOM BIRD DESIGN's Team